One Day at a Time 2017:

A husband and wife's 87-day road trip

through 22 states in the US

on two Harley Softails.

Written by: Hollie Bell-Schinzing

Copy Editor: Margarita Martinez

Book Cover Design: Joshua Bell-Schinzing

All photos supplied by the author

Publisher: Hollie Bell-Schinzing

ISBN-13: 978-0692979280 (Hollie Bell-Schinzing)

I would like to thank my husband Bonz for traveling all over the US with me and our children for their constant support of their crazy parents. I would also like to thank all the wonderful people we met along the way for being so helpful and friendly, and last but not least all my Facebook friends that followed along daily on our trip, and all their fun comments.

Contents

Introduction

Some people are planners, and others do better by running by the seat of their pants. It seems that I am better at the second option. We left home on May 31st, and returned home on Aug 26th. As it turns out, we rode through the south during the rainy season, hit the Gulf Coast for tornado season, the desert in July, and got to Colorado just in time for the monsoon season. Had I known all this in advance, I might have been a little nervous. Luckily, with the lack of this information, we just took it one day at a time and enjoyed every crazy second of our journey.

Our children are grown and have moved out of the house off on their own adventures, and I have been having issues with this change. Changing gears and purposes is not always easy for us. The house is so empty, and after so many years of taking care of children, finding things to fill my life that are not all chores is much more difficult than I thought it would be. My husband Bonz retired a year before our trip, and this is a big change for him also. I am 10 (actually nine and a half to the day) years younger than Bonz, so I don't get the option of retirement for quite some time. This is a journey of acceptance and change. Acceptance means getting to the other side. It means sorting through the feelings that interfere with integrating change, learning to be okay with the big changes coming up in our lives, and turning our focus back to what we can do instead of what we can't.

I found that after many years of marriage, you can kind of sink into a rut. After so many years of taking care of the "have to's" in busy family life, there is a divide that creeps in slowly, and you never see this until there is no one left but the two of you. Don't get me wrong. I love my husband, and I truly believe he loves me. We successfully co-exist and raised a beautiful family together, and we hardly ever fight. But reconnecting is a little harder than just wanting it. We decided that we needed something to get to know each other again, and we both love to ride motorcycles. This country is huge, and there is so much to see, we decided to take a trip around the country on our bikes, just him and I. I requested three months off work (with no pay), and my employer was gracious enough to allow this. So that was it. In June, July, and August of 2017, off we went to discover not only the USA but also ourselves.

There is a freedom that is hard to explain to people that have never ridden on a motorcycle. Your destination and distance are controlled not only by the weather, but can change at the drop of a hat when you are riding by something that looks interesting. There truly is a brotherhood between bikers that allows you to meet people wherever you go. Total strangers will come up to you and ask about your journey, and happily tell you about their experiences with their current or past motorcycle journeys. It is always easy to spot a long-distance motorcycle rider by the packs tied down to the bike or the trailers pulled behind them. You can meet fellow travelers on the road for a day or two and become lifelong friends, especially with today's technology.

Our journey took us through twenty-two states, many national parks and national monuments, and to two very popular bike rallies, one fairly new and one that has been going on for 77 years. Most of my friends call it a trip of a lifetime, but personally, I hope it is just the first long journey of many. I hope you enjoy traveling along with us on this wonderful journey to discover the wonder that this big beautiful country has to offer.

Preparing for the trip – Fairport, NY
(4/4/2017)

Following my dreams …

Your dreams are not designed to make others' eyes light up, they are designed to make your eyes light up. This is why they are called your dreams.

My children are all grown up and moved out of the house. All my "adulting" duties are done. A new phase of life is peeking its sweet little face around the corner at me and I am so excited to see it coming. That phase that we pretended to be in when we were teenagers, but could not afford to actually live, once we left our parents' house? That phase is total freedom! Today, I have the ability to make the choices I want and take the chances I choose. That phase is also known to others as retirement. I am so very excited. My husband retired last year, and I don't get to retire for a few more years, but I am close enough to feel the need to practice, and everyone knows practice makes perfect.

On May 31st, 2017, my best friend, my husband Bonz and I are hopping on our Harleys and heading down the road to wherever we end up. We don't have to be back to "adulting" until September 5th. I have already packed all the camping gear that will fit in one duffel bag. It has been sitting in my room collecting dust since January.

I thought it would be fun to start a journal for our amazing trip, so this is the prequel, in case anyone else is interested in following our adventures. Make yourself comfortable and join us for the ride of a lifetime, one day at a time.

57 days to go, but who's counting?

Day One – Sandusky, Ohio
(5/31/2017)

Today was a good day! The weather was perfect for a ride, even if the weatherman was calling for rain right up until this morning. We hit about five raindrops outside of Buffalo, just for luck. Bonz and I got a late start, but that is what happens when I sleep late, and isn't that what vacations are all about? It was a bit windy, so we rode at an 80-degree angle for a little while, but with the lack of traffic on the interstate, most of the way life was good.

We got settled in at the house (we rent the same house every year for Bike Week) and headed out to our favorite diner for dinner, Dianne's Deli and Restaurant. We have never had a bad meal there. It is usually a very fun place late at night with all the Colossalcon costumes mixed with all the biker apparel, but I didn't think the costumes started till tomorrow. (Colossalcon is an anime, gaming, and Japanese culture convention taking place at the same time as Bike Week every year in Sandusky). The sandwich Bonz ordered was huge and Bonz could not finish it, and anyone who knows my husband knows that life is all about the food! That could have something to do with his wife's lack of culinary skills, but who's counting?

Day Two – Sandusky, Ohio
(6/1/2017)

We woke up this morning about 7:00 a.m. to the sound of a jackhammer. When I looked out the window to make sure the bikes were okay, I realized it was the men working on the road right in front of our cottage, about seven feet from our bedroom window. I guess it was just my time to get up and make coffee for the crew. Kathy and Dave did not get into Sandusky until 2:00 a.m., because Dave was a little busy yesterday building a house before he left (inside joke). I figured they would be sleeping in, but by the time the coffee was brewed, the whole house was up, thanks to the lovely sound coming from the road. No worries. When you're on vacation, there is no bitching allowed.

We rent our cottage from John "The mayor of Curran Street." He literally had his own personal war on drugs and took back Currin Street from the disaster that drugs leave behind. Drugs have ruined so many lives in these United States for so long, it is really nice to hear a success story. He chased the dealers off the street by putting tacks and nails in the street. The buyers would drive down the street to buy drugs and by the time they left, their tires would be flat, and John would just pick up the phone and call the police.

They started arresting all the dealers' customers for possession, and eventually the dealers left too. But they did not leave easily. John had to send his wife and kids out of town for a little while after he heard there was a hit put out on his life. So instead of leaving, he sat on his front porch all night with a shotgun in his lap. Waiting for them to come and get him.
John is one of the nicest guys I have ever had the pleasure to meet. It is truly amazing how one person can make such a huge difference in a city like Sandusky. By taking back his street and

making it safe for his family to live here, and working with a few of his friends, the abandoned houses have, one by one, been bought and remodeled. John has handled renting out these beautifully remodeled houses for the owners for years, and now Currin Street and the streets around Currin Street are prime real estate in Sandusky, Ohio. It is so amazing how the actions of one man can make such a difference in so many lives, just for having the balls to stand up for what he believed in. He could have just walked away as all his neighbors did and allowed Currin Street to continue to be known as Crack Alley and be boarded up like so many others on this street, but he just wasn't ready to allow the ugly in this world to win and to take his house too.

When the bikers started coming by to rent his houses, he was a little nervous; I know we were one of those people in the beginning. But to talk to him today, you would never know this. He is willing to accept people for who they are and has learned a lot about the biker culture and history. And now he has many motorcycles parked up and down Currin Street for this awesome week known as Ohio Bike week. Love, honor, and respect to you, John, and thank you for allowing us to share in a small part of your dream. It is beautiful.

We headed back to our favorite diner for breakfast with Dave and Kathy before hitting the Aldi's to grab some groceries for the weekend. After we put everything away, we rode down to Mad River Harley Davidson to check out all the vendors and pick up an events calendar so we did not miss any of the fun that is planned for the rest of this week. We ran into a few people we have come to call friends that we see here every year, before heading back to the house to get a quick nap and allow Bonz to feed us some hots and burgers on the charcoal grill. The weather was unbelievably awesome today. So glad the weatherman was wrong again.

We are now heading out to the block party downtown to check out the awesome music and see if I can get away with not buy anything from any of the vendors, as there is no more room on the bike to carry it when we leave. Traditionally, Bike Week is like Christmas—streets full of vendors selling just the kind of things I like to buy. In the end, the only things I could buy today were a few stickers for my helmet, and I also collected my hog pin from the pin stop at the Harley truck, as it fits in my purse. This not shopping is going to kill me!

Day Three – Sandusky, Ohio
(6/2/2017)

Today was another great day at Bike Week. The weather was perfect again, and we started with the big breakfast at our tiki hut, thanks to my awesome husband's cooking skills. By the time we cleaned up, my cousin Laura and her husband Steve had ridden in from Indiana to join us. We all had a busy day between checking out the festivities at Margaretville and Mad River Harley Davidson, but the sun was a little intense, so we decided a nice ride out to the lighthouse in Marblehead would be much more enjoyable. The roads there are all back roads and the view is beautiful. It winds up a lake road with very little traffic, excluding the motorcycles that are there for Bike Week too.

We headed back home around 8:00 for dinner; we had thrown a roast in the crockpot before we left, so it was ready and waiting for us. Dinner was awesome, but the cold I have been pretending I don't have has decided it needs a little more attention than I have been giving it. So Dave and Kathy ran out to Walmart to get me some drugs, and now I am heading to bed as they head out to the block party downtown. Downtown Sandusky is blocked off to all traffic except motorcycles, filled with bands, people, and vendors, and is always a fun time. All in all, another great day at Bike Week!

Day Four – Putin Bay and Sandusky, Ohio
(6/3/2017)

I woke up this morning feeling so much better. I tried some baking soda and water last night before bed, to go with the drugs Dave and Kathy picked up for me. Tasted like crap, but worked wonders. Who would have guessed? Hey, I read it on the "Internets," so it must be true!

We enjoyed another big breakfast at the tiki bar before Laura and Steve headed home. We don't see enough of each other, so it really was so awesome for them to ride all the way down here to join us. I had a great time catching up. Maybe next year they can stay longer (hint hint).

It was another perfect day in Ohio, so we decided to take the ferry out to Putin Bay for the day. This was my bike's first boat ride, and it did very well (insert - proud momma). We took a ride around the whole island before stopping for some ice cream. It took us about 20 minutes because the roads are full of golf carts, and they don't move very fast. What can I say? It's a small island. I don't think I saw any speed limit signs, but the speeds of the golf carts seem to dictate the traffic, so it doesn't seem to need any.

We did find a campground on the island, and had to ride through to check it out. With all the beautiful houses, I did not expect to find camping, but just as everything else on the island, the campground was striking. We also found a cute little park overlooking all the boats and yachts. They even have a water taxi to bring in the people on and off the yachts when they want to come to land, because the dock is not large enough for some of those beasts.

We did meet the owner of the hardware store's dad, and had a wonderful conversation about what it is like to live on this beautiful island all year long. There are about 300 permanent residents and when the lake freezes, the ferry no longer runs. So the locals have to fly in and out to reach the mainland in the winter. He also said that you had better have at least two freezers and stock them up to make it through the winter. Their high school graduating class is also very small; I believe he said it was five students last year. We thanked him for all the wonderful information he shared with us and headed out to see what else we could discover on this beautiful island.

Anyone who has ever gone out to Putin Bay will know that a stop at the roundhouse to watch Mad Dog play is just necessary. He has been playing there forever! He can put on quite a show. He's a little bit comedian and a little bit musician and a lot of bit entertainer and can really get the crowd going. The place is always packed when he plays. We could have stayed longer, but the last ferry was at 6:00 p.m. if we wanted to get the bikes back across the lake, so off we went to give our bikes their second boat trip.

Back at Margaretville, we said our goodbyes to Magnetic Mike, and exchanged phone numbers as he will be in northern Colorado around the same time as us, so we hope to see him in a few months. We headed back to the block party to watch our favorite band, The Earthquakers. They are four guys on stage dressed like Amish guys with the shorts, suspenders, and Amish hats. The first time we saw them up on stage at Bike Week, they looked so out of place, but then they started to play ... and man, can they play! You have to watch the drummer; he is quite entertaining. The show tonight was as awesome, as always.

Saturday night at Bike Week is a little depressing; tomorrow everyone packs up and heads home. We give the city of Sandusky back to the people who live here, and all the bikes slowly drift back out of town. Last year it ended with quite a bang; two tornadoes hit two hours after we left. And we rode home through that storm. We knew it was ugly, but did not realize how ugly until we saw the news the next day.

But traditionally, we always hit rain either on the way in or on the way out. But the weekend is always worth it. Hopefully we can head out early enough to miss the thunderstorms tomorrow. It looks like Dave and Kathy will hit the storms in Buffalo as they head back to Rochester, but we are heading south, so we have a chance of missing it altogether.

Day Five – Findlay, Ohio
(6/4/2017)

Today was a little rough. We got up and checked the weather app on my phone, and according to it, the rain was coming between 9:00 a.m. and 10:00 a.m. (and it did), but then there was a five-hour window for us to get south to miss the thunderstorms for today. After packing everything up and making sure everything was in order at the house, we headed out around 11. Leaving Sandusky on Sunday is always a little melancholy, as we know we won't be back for another year. Kathy and Dave headed out at the same time and headed back to Rochester; the weather that way looked even worse.

We made it to the end of the street before I told Bonz he needed to stop. The bags on his bike were really leaning to the right and I wanted to check them again. I tightened up the ties holding them down and the heat and humidity were killer while we were stopped, especially since we had way too many clothes on (boots, jeans, chaps, and coats because we were expecting rain). We took off and made it a few miles before we had to pull over again because the bags were moving to the right again after each bump in the road. He stopped at a convenience store and I pulled them completely off the bike and re-tied them down.

I am usually the Packing Queen, but we are trying something new this trip. Instead of the multiple bungee cords I usually use, we are using two ratchet straps per bike. As I have never really used these before, I am learning that I suck at using them, which may be obvious from having to tie down his bike three times before we even got out of Sandusky. After about 20 minutes of actually riding ... we had to pull over again as the camping bag on my bike had way too much weight on the right side and had me going down the road at an 80-degree angle on the straight sections of the road.

We pulled into an empty parking lot and I tried to repack the bag to get the weight right but couldn't do it without dropping some of the weight in the bag. So the extra tent and blowup mattress had to go (Bonz called it his master suite). So you could say I dropped 40 pounds at the 500-mile mark of our trip. What a huge difference. My bike was so very happy. Bonz said he would just stock up on Breathe Rite strips (because for some reason he thinks that I snore).

The ride was going great, no rain so far and the humidity was not nearly as bad at 70 mph, until we stopped for gas about 16 miles out of Findley, Ohio, and realized how utterly shot we both were. I was searching my phone to try and find a hotel, as the thunderstorms were expected overnight, and the sweetest couple overheard us talking and stopped next to us. They told us our best bet would be the Country Inn and Suites in Findley, Ohio. They said that they had taken very good care of them a few years ago when they stayed there during a tornado. They gave us directions and we decided that today could be a day of rest.

Not sure if it is the cold I am coming down with (which I refuse to acknowledge); staying out till two at the block party last night (because I'm old); or re-tying down the bags in the humidity three times (which actually took a total of two and a half hours); but I was so very ready for a nap. We checked in and got all the bags into the room, and took a look out the window at the rain coming down in sheets. The app on my phone said we had another three hours before the rain hit. I guess we made the right decision. And my nap was awesome!

When we got there and were unpacking the bikes, we met another nice man who came over and started talking to us. He owned a GoldWing and had just lost his wife a few months back in Florida. He was from Ohio, had a date with an old flame tonight, and was waiting on her arrival. I love how when we travel on bikes, so many people will be so friendly. If we showed up in a car, we never would have had the pleasure of meeting the wonderful people we have.

Our GoldWing friend recommended a restaurant across the road, and when Bonz got up from his nap we realized that the only thing we had eaten all day was a banana from the convenience store in Sandusky. So we headed over to the Beer and Barrel Pizza and Grill, and we found that our GoldWing friend was totally correct. Both the food and service were very good, and now I think it is time for a slightly longer nap.

Day Six – Florence, Kentucky
(6/5/2017)

Today was a good day. Slept late and did the breakfast at the hotel, and returned my crown to my head, because all girls need a tiara! I am again the Packing Queen; we will call yesterday a training day. (LOL) We did not get that many miles under our belt today as we caught up to the thunderstorms in West Chester, Ohio, and they were not moving very fast. The day had been perfect for riding up until then, but the closer we got to our destination, the darker the sky got. It looked pretty cool, lightning to the left and black skies, and blue skies to the right, until the road made a left-hand curve right into the black sky.

We spent about an hour and a half waiting at a Dunkin' Donuts, twenty minutes from Cincinnati!! Now, anyone that knows Bonz knows that Cincinnati chili is his most favorite meal in the world, and he loves his food. Not only has he talked about it for the last 30 years, but he also cooks one hell of a chili. The only thing he hates enough to wait a few more hours to eat Cincinnati chili is riding through thunderstorms. So we waited. When we headed out, we hit rush hour traffic, so we were speeding down the road for about 20 miles at a racecar speed of five mph (or should I say go-cart speed). But that's okay, because we actually made it to Chili Time on Vine, and it was definitely worth the wait!

Yep, I am now a true Cincinnati chili convert. The staff was awesome, and made us feel right at home. By the time we left, we felt like we were leaving friends behind. After a meal like that, we decided to grab a room after we hit Kentucky. Our new friends at Chili Time suggested finding one on online, so we downloaded the app for TripAdvisor and found a fairly decent room for $52 for the night (with breakfast). Not knowing the town, we pulled into the parking lot to check it out first, before I placed the order online.

So far, we have met about five different people staying here because they are working in the area, two iron workers, and a car salesman who travels all over and helps re-design the layout of the showrooms for different dealerships. So far, we love Kentucky. Tomorrow, we are headed to Lexington for a play day, so tonight I am taking two nighttime cold pills for this croupy cough that I seem to have from the cold that I refuse to admit I have.

Day Seven – Versailles, Kentucky
(6/6/2017)

Another beautiful day. We overslept for breakfast, but had time for a cup of coffee. Getting quicker at tying up the bikes, but the next trip I hope to only pack a credit card. It would save a lot of time and energy! We have been getting to bed late every night and therefore sleeping in in the morning, and I think we need to get some earlier starts to our day.

We called the Kentucky Horse Park but realized we needed to make the reservation at least 24 hours in advance, so I found another campground in Versailles, about 18 miles out of Lexington. It is a cute place, just a campground with a circle in the middle, and camping to the right of the road. The sites are cheap, $20 a night with electric, but I have not found the water for coffee yet. I think we need to get it from the washroom area and carry it back. As the campsite is so small, it is not a far walk.

The campsite is in the middle of nowhere, and down a long windy road, which makes for a nice ride. After setting up, Bonz is taking a nap. I think he is now coming down with the cold I refuse to admit I have. He, on the other hand, is a little more willing to admit he is sick. We have the site for two days, and think today is a good day to be lazy and sleep this stupid cold away; it is slowing us right down to a crawl. I have no Internet at this site, so I think this post may be delayed until tomorrow. Neither my phone nor the T-Mobile hot spot work here. (I'm such a geek!)

On our way through Lexington, we passed the Kingsland Horse Farm. Wow, it is huge, and absolutely gorgeous from the road, and I think we may need to take a quick putt through tomorrow. It is the largest stables in Lexington and the most beautiful. Right after the track is a huge castle built on top of a hill (could be where the name came from) with black wrought iron gates that you need to pass through to get to it (of course, the gate was closed, so a putt through there is most likely unadvised). I mean a real castle with turrets and everything!

When talking to the locals, they say the castle is full of mysterious rumors. According to the rumors, a slew of celebrities has owned it, including Lee Majors and Burt Reynolds. The truth is that the property is up for sale at 30,000,000. At present, it is a working inn. I would have stopped for a picture but there was a truck right behind me and I did not feel like being squished like the bugs on my windshield. I found out this morning that the campsite does have Wi-Fi. Sometimes it pays to ask. It just does not work in our area of the campsite yet. Bonz's impression of sleeping in the tent was, "I have a big old house, and a camper; remind me why we are sleeping in a tent?" As it turns out, the blow-up mattress that we kept has a slow leak in it, so we kept waking up and having to fill it with air again. Thank God, we decided to get the spot with electric. And I did pretty good at figuring out how to use the teeny tiny stove I bought to make coffee, so life is good again.

Day Eight – Versailles, Kentucky
(6/7/2017)

Today was a little colder than the other days. It was 66 degrees by midafternoon. We heard a weird animal sound in the middle if the night. It actually sounded more like an elk, but they don't have them in this area. All I know is it was NOT a bear. Yes, Bonz, NOT a bear, but they do have bears in this area. I successfully accomplished making coffee, so the stars are aligned correctly. Spent the morning talking to the camp manager's wife and headed on out to view the sights. She also thinks it was not a bear, as they have not seen any in the camp yet.

First stop, brunch! Stopped at a little place called Melissa's and had a whole bunch of goodness. Melissa's Hot Brown is an open-faced roasted turkey and ham sandwich smothered with Mornay sauce and peppercorn cheese, topped with bacon and broiled to perfection. This was most likely a week's worth of calories, but worth every bite!

When we left there, we stopped at the hardware store to grab a patch for the mattress, so I don't have to keep blowing it up all night. My friend from our HOG group, Maureen, suggested the Bourbon Trail and seeing Bardstown, so off we headed. We got sidetracked by the Wild Turkey distillery sign at an exit on the way, and being that I was known to light up many a bar's surface with flaming shots of Wild Turkey back in the day, we pulled off and followed the signs there. It was a little after two when we got there and the tour was at three, so we decided to wait and take the tour. It was very informative, and people loved us, as we gave all our shots away at the end. I guess most people on these tours drink. (Can't imagine why I would think that; it is a bourbon factory after all).

After smelling the bourbon at the distillery, we decided that a quick stop at the Urgent Care in Versailles was probably a really good idea, as the cold that I refuse to admit I have has now blossomed into a beautiful case of bronchitis, and Bonz is catching it too. So they saw us both, and sent us on our way with a couple of prescriptions. Needless to say, we never made it all the way to Bardstown today.

When we got back to camp, we decided it would be a good idea to stay one more day and let the drugs kick in. If you ever want a great place to stay in Kentucky, with great people in a quaint little campsite, I highly recommend Camp on the Kentucky. So, depending on how we feel tomorrow, we will either be out gallivanting again or watching Netflix up on the camp store porch, as that is where the Wi-Fi works.

Day Nine – Versailles, Kentucky
(6/8/2017)

Well, today was an official sick day. I slept till 11:00 a.m., got up made coffee, and went back to bed till 1:30. Not even enough energy to watch Netflix on the porch. Bonz started a new book and I read a little between naps. Around 2:00, we decided to head to Wally World (Walmart) to get a new blow-up mattress, as waking up on the ground every few hours, and pumping the mattress back up, was not helping. We headed out, following the Garmin's directions, and it took us down the most beautiful winding and twisty road. Even the bridge over the Kentucky River had a twist to it. This area is absolutely gorgeous!

We did not stay long at Wally World, just picked up a few subs and a mattress and headed back down the most beautiful 11 miles back to camp. We really are out in the middle of nowhere, camped right on the bank of the Kentucky River, but surrounded in beauty. I could not ask for a more beautiful place to feel so yucky.

The plan is to head out tomorrow and put some miles in. As it is Bonz and Lindsey's birthday tomorrow, we will be stopping to call our daughter Lindsey and grab a hotel room and a good meal to celebrate Bonz's wonderful day. Hopefully, we both will be feeling better by then. In the meantime, I am headed back to bed for a much-needed nap.

Day Ten – Nashville, Tennessee
(6/9/17)

Another beautiful day for a ride. Rode the Blue Ridge Parkway most of the way down to Nashville, and passed the 1000-mile mark on the bikes before we got here. For some reason, Bonz's bike has 17 more miles than me for this trip, and we can't figure out how. He says it is because he rides in the front. I say, God help me, I married my dad!

We had planned to ride to Bardstown on the Bourbon Trail the day we visited the Wild Turkey Distillery, but never made it. As we were heading down the Blue Ridge Parkway, we saw an exit for Bardstown. My girlfriend Maureen from our HOG group had great things to say about the town, so we were pretty pleased to be able to see it. We stopped at Mammy's Kitchen and had some of the best chicken fried chicken, with homemade mashed potatoes smothered in a white cream sauce, that I have ever tasted. Oh, yeah, there were green beans and a roll too. The town was pretty cool, and we will have to come back again someday when we have more time to enjoy it. Thanks, Maureen, for the great recommendation!

We met a nice couple riding in from Illinois, near the Tennessee border, for a Widows Sons Masonic Riders Association gathering. He let me sit on his dresser and I think I am in love. That seat alone was awesome! So was the rest of the bike, with all the bells and whistles. I do have to say, Harley gets better every year.

I tried using TripAdvisor again, but I don't think it went through. We tried to book a room at the Knights Inn in downtown Nashville, when we were an hour out of town. When we got there, the guy at the desk was awesome and gave us the discount anyway. He gave us a ground floor room with a view of the parking for the bikes. They get five stars just for that! We are in the city, but not as close to everything as I thought, but a quick cab ride downtown can take care of that.

After a nice call with my daughter for her birthday, we headed into town to celebrate Bonz's birthday. It turns out that tonight is the CMA Awards night, the busiest night of the year in Nashville. Luckily, we took a cab there and back. We stopped at a few of the bars on Broadway to watch the bands. They even have a Margaretville here too! But the original one is in Ohio (at least that is what their name said). Checked out Crazy Town, The Fiddler's Inn, and a few more I don't remember the names of. What a great place to people watch! It's my favorite hobby.

Day Eleven – Nashville, Tennessee
(6/10/17)

Another beautiful hot day in Nashville. Started our day at the Soap Opry Laundromat and met many nice people there. It was actually a fun place to be this morning. I usually hate laundromats, but they can be fun when you are on vacation. I guess it is all in the attitude. When we got back to the room, it was too hot to head out, so I went to the pool to swim for a bit. The hotel has a beautiful outdoor pool and it breaks my heart to see it not being used.

Around 2:00 p.m., we headed out to try to find the Grand Old Opry Hotel, as my friend Laurie said the place was "a city within itself" and she was not kidding. You can take a boat ride through the inside of the hotel in a huge lazy river that runs through the hotel. There are islands and bridges and buildings built within the building. Not to mention the many restaurants and shops lined along the hallways. It was absolutely beautiful; I would like to someday meet the person who came up with such an unusual idea. I have always been fascinated by the unusual.

We stopped at one of the restaurants for lunch and it was pretty good, for an overpriced hotel restaurant. I definitely prefer the atmosphere of a small family-owned restaurant to the crisp atmosphere of a corporate run restaurant. I guess after all the beauty of the hotel, I was expecting more, but Bonz was pretty impressed with the multiple TVs in the men's room. We were going to visit the Opry House, but there is a concert there tonight, so we did not think we could get in, as it was getting late.

We headed back to the hotel and watched a pretty good movie on HBO—*The Accountant*, with Ben Affleck. We are both feeling better than we were the other day, but not quite fully up to par, so a nice night in the air conditioning is just what the doctor ordered. We are leaving tomorrow morning, as we are expecting three to five days of thunderstorms starting Monday or Tuesday and want to ride the Dragon on a nice day.

Day Twelve – Kingston, Tennessee
(6/11/2017)

Another hot, hot day for riding. It was already in the 80s when we left. Packed up in the sun and hit the road. The helmet communicators quit working again not far from the motel, and that meant I had to take the lead again. So far, we have done a lot of interstate riding; Tennessee is a beautiful state with all the mountains and curving roads. But the interstate is direct sun all the way. Not too bad when we are moving, but about 100 miles into the trip the traffic came to a crawl because of a bad accident. Traffic was backed up for a little more than two mountains.

When we got past the accident, we pulled over at the next rest area to get some water. We found a nice picnic table in the shade and I pulled up a YouTube video on how to repair the head sets. I absolutely love YouTube! Bonz is back in the lead, and we are no longer lost! Met another biker at the rest area; he was headed to Boston. We seem to meet more and more long-distance riders lately. It used to be very rare, but not so much anymore.

About 50 miles later, we stopped for lunch in Crossville, Tennessee, at Rio's Country Kitchen. They just opened up three weeks ago, and if you are ever near there I highly recommend it. Another fabulous southern meal of chicken fried steak with mashed potato casserole. Yep, I'm definitely in love with southern cooking. We even met a woman from Rochester, NY, when we were leaving the restaurant. We had a nice conversation and she said she absolutely loves living in the south. I am starting to understand why; the food alone could make you want to stay. I'm sure the weather helps too.

In Kingston, Tennessee, we pulled over for gas, and when we stopped I realized that the sun was just kicking my ass again. So we checked the TripAdvisor app, found a motel about a half mile down the road, and decided we were done for the day. The Lakeview Inn is a very cute little motel, and will make a perfect new home for us tonight. They gave us a room on the first floor and again get five stars just for that. There is the cutest Mexican restaurant right next door, and it was calling Bonz's name, so off we went to eat again. If we keep up this pace, I may just have to lose the camping gear to fit all my new weight that I am collecting eating all this awesome southern food! Yep, today was a full day of riding, meeting great people, and eating. I will give it a 10 for the day.

Day Thirteen – Robbinsville, North Carolina
(6/12/2017)

Today was a biker's dream. We woke up about 8:00 a.m. and the weatherman said it was going to be "another tropical day." I-40 East was a quarter mile away and our destination was about two hours away. I just could not do it. We decided to get lost instead. So we headed in the wrong direction and found a nice backroad to get lost on. I do not think they know how to build a straight road in this area.

We set the Garmin to Tellico Plains, Tennessee, and made it recalculate many times, as it kept trying to bring us back on I-40 East. One advantage to using a cheap Garmin on the bike is not listening to her saying "recalculating" multiple times. Saw some great views from the backroads. We were heading to the Tail of the Dragon, and the site I looked up said it started in Tellico Plains. I checked the Garmin for the Dragon and nothing was coming up, but I did find Cherohala Motorcycle resort in Tellico Plains, TN, so we set that as our destination and went to get lost.

When we got to the motorcycle resort, it was a campground with cute cabins. Very adorable spot, but the owner was off running errands and left a number for anyone to call if they needed them. I did not feel it was a good idea to bug them for directions, so I plugged in the nearest gas station, as they are always good for directions. There was no cell phone service at the campsite, so it was great to have the Garmin working.

We met a few people at the gas station and they gave us directions to the Charles Hall Museum down the road, as they have maps and cater to bikers. The gentleman we were talking to also warned us that seven people have died on the Dragon this year alone. I thanked them for the directions and headed off to the museum.

The visitor's center and museum were in the same parking lot and the museum is actually a store full of biker stuff! T-shirts, pins, shot glasses, etc. The gentleman that was working was very helpful to a lost soul like me. We had already been riding for a couple of hours to get where we were. He explained that the Dragon was just down the road a bit and to take the Cherohala Skyway to 129 and take a left on 129. Having not done any research on the subject, I did not realize we were about to enter the most beautiful road I have ever ridden, with many scenic overlooks to admire the view.

The "Cherohala Skyway is 43-miles long and connects Tellico Plains, Tennessee, with Robbinsville, North Carolina. It opened in the fall of 1996. The highway starts at 800 ft. in elevation and climbs over mountains as high as 5390 ft. at Santeetlah Overlook on the state border. Twenty-one miles of the Skyway are in southeast Tennessee and fifteen miles of it are in North Carolina. The road crosses through the Cherokee and Nantahala National Forests, thus the name "Chero ... hala." The National Scenic Byway is beautiful mountain views of the Cherokee National Forest and the Telco River. It is one of the most beautiful roads I have ever ridden.

Around 4:00 p.m., we pulled into a cute little country store, Thunder Mountain General Store and Deli. It even had a sign on the porch that said "Please do not pee off the porch". It turns out this store is often seen on the Discovery Channel show *Moonshiners*. I love unique stores like this, and we enjoyed the best homemade cinnamon buns I have had since my mom used to make them when I was a kid. We met a wonderful couple from Texas; they were staying at a campsite near there. Bonz got into a nice conversation with the general store owner and he suggested a room at the Two Wheeled Inn, and said they even had a garage for the bikes with every room. Well, not only was I getting ready to quit for today, but the suggestion just sounded like way too much fun, so off we went.

When we got to the motel, the owner showed us our room and garage. The garage door opener is inside the room next to the door. Inside the garage is our own hot water heater, two chairs to sit outside our room and visit with all the other people who are staying here, and rags to wash the bikes! I was in love before I even saw the room! The room has a king-sized bed, desk, and an oversized shower in the bathroom. Now I am never leaving.

We got the room for two days, with the ability to stay longer if we want. The weatherman says that they are expecting five days of thunderstorms in the south (everywhere we planned to go) and according to everyone we spoke to, they usually get thunderstorms between 2:00 and 4:00 every day. Then everything including the roads dry up. I think this is the perfect place to wait the storm out. And to top it all off, there is a steakhouse next door that serves breakfast. Because when you travel with Bonz, it is all about the food!

We hung outside for a little bit, meeting our new neighbors, before we headed next door to eat. It turns out this is a dry county in the middle of the Bible Belt, and the steakhouse is the only place that sells alcohol. Not that that matters to us, but it came up in a conversation about the two tennis courts, one in front and one in back of the restaurant. It turns out that the tennis courts and the horse barn were necessary to get a permit to sell alcohol on the premise. Every state has its weird laws, and sometimes they do not make sense to me. I have never, in all my years of riding, seen bikers riding to the tennis court. (Except Georgia! Bring your racket when you come here, girl).

Well, I am going to get some sleep and try and hit the Dragon tomorrow, as it got too late to do it today.

Day Fourteen – Robbinsville, North Carolina
(6/13/17)

This morning was a sad day. When I got up at 7:00 a.m. and walked outside, everything was covered in a beautiful thick fog. This explains the name the Smoky Mountains. My thoughts were back home today. Our roommate Gary has been watching our dog, cat, and house while we are gone. Momma, our cat, tripped our dog the other day.

Tala, our dog, has always had issues with her back legs, and was born with the issue. She has not gotten up in a few days and has quit eating and drinking. Gary has been doing what he can to keep her comfortable, but she is not getting any better. He is calling her vet today, and I do not expect good news. I feel very bad for not being there at this time of her life, and am very grateful for Gary's kindness at this time. She has been a good dog over the last 12 years, and it will be very weird when we get home and she is not there to let in and out whenever anyone goes near a door. And who will eat all the candy in the hidden Easter baskets before the kids get up? She will definitely be missed.

By the time we got moving today and headed over to the steakhouse for breakfast, we were too late, as it was already 11:00 a.m. and they stop serving breakfast at 10:00. So we saddled up and headed out to the Huddle House for breakfast. We were met at the door by the owner and told they were closed because they were waiting for more help to show up, and would be serving again in another half hour. Bonz waits for no man when he's hungry, so we saw that Bojangles down the road served breakfast too, but when we got there their fried chicken looked too good to pass up. So we enjoyed a great breakfast of fried chicken and mashed potatoes with gravy. Did I tell you how much I love southern cooking? Can't get frustrated when you're on vacation, but when it is messing with my honey's tummy ...Very scary.

We met a couple before we headed out and they told us the headline in the paper today said another two people got killed on the Dragon yesterday. I don't know why people feel the need to spread bad news like that after you say that is where you are headed. We thanked them and, with a full tummy and a smile back on Bonz's face, we saddled back up and headed out to the Dragon, slightly more nervous than we were before we left.

The Dragon is about 18 miles down Route 129, another beautiful winding road. We stopped at Deals Gap motorcycle resort, which is the last stop before you hit the Dragon. Met another nice couple there, and his bike was at the shop for the day. It needed a part because the battery would not re-charge, so they were riding double on her bike, and she was really regretting her choice in backseats.

Slightly nervous, we headed off through the Dragon's Tail. I told Bonz we needed to just do this once and then we could check it off the bucket list. There were 318 turns in 11 miles. There were pull offs along the way to let faster cars and bikes go by if you like, and I liked a lot. As you couldn't see very far ahead or behind, some of those crotch rockets and cars just quickly showed up behind you with no warning, and it was just safer to let them pass.

We were all there to enjoy the ride, and there were many styles of riding. Some were into speed, and some (like me) just like to putt. My goal was to make it to the other end alive, as it was not a very good day to die, and letting them pass allowed them to enjoy their style too. There was one scenic overlook on the Dragon and we stopped there to say a prayer for my friend Dianne, as her late husband's ashes were spread there. We took the curves one at a time and before you knew it, we were done with the Dragon. Just as in life, if you break it into little pieces when things seem to overwhelm you, you can make it to the other end with a lot less stress.
It is funny, as soon as we left the Dragon on the Tennessee side, we were on the straightest road I had seen in days! 129 on the other side of the Dragon wrapped around the lake in very slow curves. We stopped at US 129 Dragon Harley Davidson, as it was the first stop we saw after the Dragon ride, and checked the map.

To get back, we had a few choices, one longer than the other, or we had to turn around and head back through the Dragon. Riding through the Smoky Mountains at night sounded a lot less appealing than going through the Dragon again. After finishing it once today and actually knowing there were not any curves that we could not make, it was a little less stressful the second time around, and a lot more enjoyable. There is power in facing things that make you nervous, or scare you. Always remember that without fear, there is no courage! If anyone is interested in riding the Tail of the Dragon, I would highly recommend trying this run at least once. It was just awesome.

Heading back from the Dragon, we decided to go back to Thunder Mountain General Store and Deli, grab some sandwiches, and thank the owner again for all his help yesterday. We made the right on Route 143 back up the mountain, and the sky opened up. Thunder and lightning was coming down in sheets, making it hard to see all the twists and turns. It felt like forever but was actually only eight miles before the store came into view. So we went in and ordered a couple awesome sandwiches and waited out the storm with the great company of the owner, his lovely wife, and daughter. Only been here a few days and they felt like family!

The store closed at six and the storm shrank to a trickle, so we mounted back up and headed the 11 miles back to our awesome room with a garage to wipe the bikes down and dry off, and rented the room for another day! Rumor had it you had to see the waterfalls on Moonshiner Trail. It is actually the route they used to use during Prohibition. What a wonderful excuse to stay another day. Not really sure if we are ever leaving here.

On the way back, the mist was coming back to the mountains. The fingers of the clouds were touching down on the mountains, and it left the effect of the mountain on fire with smoke billowing up to the sky. What a gorgeous picture that would have made if I could have captured it in a picture, but I'm not that good with a camera at 50 mph.

Day Fifteen – Robbinsville, North Carolina
(6/14/17)

We spent the morning on the phone with Gary, our roommate, and Bro Joe. They are putting Tala, our dog, down today. She was a good dog and will be missed. It is funny how animals can worm their way into your heart in their short lives and truly become a part of your family. It is hard to let them go, but the joy they bring into your life far outweighs the sadness you feel when they leave.

We stayed in and watched TV today. Got caught up on *Orange is the New Black*, until Bonz got hungry and we had to venture out, as there was nothing to eat in the room. We stopped at the local secondhand shop, as I love to treasure hunt in them, especially when we are out of town. It is kind of like antiquing, only cheaper. You never know what you can find. I found the cutest little Hog statue, and thought it would look cute in the office of the inn, so I picked it up for Linda, as she has been very accommodating to us during our stay here. I also checked the weather in Helen, Georgia, again and guess what … They are expecting more thunder storms. So we decided to stay one more day. Yep. We are never leaving here, but it's a great place to get stuck.

Rumor had it that the local grocery store has the best fried chicken in town, so we had to check it out, and, yes, it was delicious. We brought dinner back to the room and visited with the other guests at the inn. The rooms are starting to fill up as the weekend is coming, and it is always fun to meet new people.

Heading back to the TV to watch some more stupid movies on cable and will check in again tomorrow.

Day Sixteen – Robbinsville, North Carolina
(6/15/17)

After our lousy cable movie ended last night, I got up to get a glass of water and found there was no water. I walked out to see if anyone was still up and found a group hanging out in the first row of the inn. Turned out that there was a water main break in town and everyone's water was out. But they were passing the peach moonshine around and enjoying a few beers. There was a group of four Canadians, a couple from Michigan, and a guy from Nebraska, hanging out telling stories and laughing. Bonz stayed in and went to sleep (as he still is under the impression that I snore, and claims to sleep better when I'm awake) so I went out and joined the party! We had lots of fun and laughs.

I headed back to the room around midnight as the Canadians and Tim from Nebraska were all heading home in the morning. I cannot imagine trying to ride all that way home with the Canadian flu (our family's description for a hangover) while having my head confined in a helmet. When I used to drink, I never seemed to get very many miles in, so now that I do not drink, this is a feeling I have no intention of ever knowing. But they were all so very funny last night, and I truly enjoyed all their company. Like Linda, the owner of the inn says, you come as guests and leave as friends; this is so true. If you ride any style of motorcycle, I highly recommend adding this little slice of heaven to your road trip list. You will not be disappointed.

We woke up this morning feeling great after relaxing all day yesterday. Sometimes you just need a nice relaxing day to give you enough energy to start attacking life again. The plan for yesterday was to check out the waterfalls along the Moonshiner Route. It is the actual route they used to use to transfer the alcohol during Prohibition (only paved now). The Moonshiners' Circle is absolutely beautiful. It wraps along the beautiful river that these days is filled with rafters shooting the current.

We pulled over to check the view and the map, and another biker pulled in. We started talking and Jeff, a local guy, offered to show us where the falls were. Life is so awesome! We now had our own personal tour guide! We spent the afternoon riding together, and Bonz and I would never have found the falls that he pointed out for us. With all the beautiful greenery growing, if you did not know where they were, you would have just ridden by.

By the time we finished the lower half, Wayah Rd (Route 1310), the sky was turning black again. We made it to Franklin for gas, and Jeff had to head home as he had to work tonight, so Bonz and I decided to have a late lunch and wait till the thunderstorm had passed. There was a café connected to the gas station and we figured we would stop for a sandwich. What a lovely surprise when we walked into a beautiful restaurant with an awesome menu. Café Rel. Turned out the chef was from the Pocono's, got tired of the rat race, moved to Franklin, North Carolina, and opened his own restaurant. The food and the atmosphere were top notch, and, of course, we enjoyed some lovely conversations with other people eating in the restaurant. Southern hospitality is alive and kicking, and truly an enjoyable phenomenon. And so was the extremely large size of the chocolate cake we ordered for desert.

After lunch, we headed up Route 28 "The Moonshiner," which is another curvy, twisty, beautiful, bending, curling, zig-zag kind of road with a beautiful view, and a lot less traffic than the Tail of the Dragon. Just as we started coiling up the mountain, the rain started again. It was not a thunderstorm, more like a shower, so we kept going. As we twisted up the mountain, we rode in and out of the rain. The weather in this area is quite different as it can be pouring one minute and a half mile away the roads are dry. Not only that, there is no such thing as a straight road, and our best bet for a weather report is to look up and ride towards the blue sky and not the black one. It is kind of a new game of storm chasing, only we are trying to ride away from the storm and not into it.

When we got back to the Inn, we now had many new neighbors. We met a nice group from Ohio and visited for a while, before we had to break off and do laundry, as our plan is to head out of our Shangri-La (earthly paradise) before we never leave. So tomorrow morning we need to be locked and loaded before 10:00, and then we are off to explore more wonderful parts of this great country.

Day Seventeen – Atlanta, Georgia
(6/16/17)

We were locked and loaded by 9:58 am. Checkout from the Two Wheel Inn was 10:00 a.m., so we were running right on time, so very unlike me. We plugged Helen, Georgia, into the GPS, and headed out to explore, and were to arrive just in time for lunch. The roads were much straighter than the roads we had been riding, but they still had a few 180-degree turns through the mountain.

Our friends Gary and Sue recommended seeing Helen before we left, since we were so close. Great choice! It is the cutest little German town with all the gingerbread trimmings on the buildings and many German restaurants and shops lining the main street. And to top it off, they even have prime motorcycle-only parking right downtown. One of the people we talked to in Robbinsville suggested going to Hoffer's Bakery and Café and said it was the best German food she ever tried, so we headed there first, of course.

The food was very good. Bonz had bratwurst and sauerkraut, and I had a pastrami sandwich. Both were very good, and no complaints. After lunch, we walked around town and checked out a few shops, and, of course, I left with a new necklace. Bonz is so good to me. I may not have lots of real estate in the bags to pack much more, but I can always find room for jewelry. Helen is a wonderful day trip, and if you are ever in the area, I highly recommend stopping by.

We reset the Garmin to New Orleans and it took us down some very nice roads. That is until we hit Atlanta, Georgia, around 4:00 p.m. It was a 10-lane parking lot. And anyone that rides an air-cooled bike knows how hot they can get idling in 90-degree weather. After a while, all I could smell was that smell you get when ironing clothes and the iron is too hot. The problem was that my legs were still in the jeans that were being ironed by the heat from my motorcycle.

We pulled off at the next exit and the traffic was not much better. I begged Bonz to make his next right and we ended up in a beautiful neighborhood lined with mansions and found a shady spot in front of a beautiful house. Life was so much better in this spot that we decided to stay there a few hours to allow traffic to at least move a little and allow my bike to cool down some. While hanging out in the shade we got to meet the neighbors, and even the UPS guy drove past us enough times to start waving as he passed. The neighbor we met said Friday rush hour traffic was always the worst and that it should let up about 7:30 p.m. But Saturday, traffic was much better.

So since we had the time, we decided to check my TripAdvisor app on my phone and found a Hampton Inn five miles in the wrong direction. Problem was, the traffic going the other way was just as bad. So, we made a reservation and continued to hang out on our new curb for a little while longer. About 6:30, we decided we better leave before the owner of the lovely house called the police on us. I did suggest setting up the tent, as the yard was so beautiful, but Bonz would not go for that.

By the time we finally made it to the Hampton Inn, 30 minutes later, that beautiful ironing smell was really getting strong again, and my poor thigh was on fire. We unloaded all but the camping gear, because at this point I really didn't care if someone stole it. It would just be less stuff I have to tie down on the bike when we head out each time. We found a parking spot for the bikes that we could see from our room, and noticed a bakery right across the parking lot, so off we went. After eating, we were both in better moods and cooled down enough to appreciate heading back to our beautiful room with the perfect bed. Life is good again!

Day Eighteen – Greenville, Alabama
(6/17/17)

Today was a perfect travel day. The thing about riding a motorcycle is that even travel days are fun. We stopped at a rest area right inside Alabama, and they were watering the lawn. I just could not help myself, so I ran through it. There was a group of Boy Scouts who had stopped for lunch, and I tried to talk them into joining me in the sprinkler, but they would not do it. I am losing my touch; I used to be able to corrupt a Boy Scout or two in my younger days. As it turns out, the sprinkler was unnecessary, as we rode right into a thunderstorm a little while later.

We pulled off at the next exit and decided it was a good time for lunch as it was going on 3:00 p.m. I am finding if we plan meals around the thunderstorms that the ride is much more pleasant, as the storms disappear within an hour and then the weather is perfect again. I had a great shrimp dish over rice, and Bonz had a shaved steak with melted cheddar cheese and garlic parmesan fries. We had pulled into the nearest restaurant from the exit. It was a LongHorn Steakhouse, and Bonz had talked about trying out that chain. I'm not real big on chain restaurants, (firm believer of buying local, especially when traveling) but this one was very good, and the location was perfect.

Around 6:00 (7:00 our time, as we are now on Central Time), we decided we had had enough, so we found a room in Greenville. We are staying at the Baymont Inn and Suites, and it is not bad for a three-star motel, but the bed is a lot harder than the luxury of the Hampton Inn last night. Sometimes those extra stars really make a difference in comfort and in price. But to be honest, Bonz is very happy because the room came with a lounge chair with an ottoman, and ShowTime is on the 32- inch flat screen TV. So Bonz is happy and life is still good!

Day Nineteen – Biloxi, Mississippi
(6/19/17)

Today was Father's Day, so we started our day Skyping with Josh, our son, and Jess, his girlfriend, in Dubai, and had a lovely call with Lindsey, our daughter, in Florida. We were locked and loaded by 11:00 a.m., and headed on down the interstate. Riding the interstate can really get boring after a while, but it's still better than going a long distance in a car. Right before exit ten on interstate 65, the road made a left-hand curve, right into the black sky that we had been barely missing all day. I tried to tell Bonz we would just ride right through it again, and just as I finished that sentence a huge bolt of lightning shrieked through the sky. So we decided it was a perfect time for lunch. We pulled into the nearest gas station in Chickasaw and asked some people getting gas where we could find a nice place to sit out the storm and have a bite to eat. They suggested the American Buffett across the street, for great southern comfort food. So off we went.

We walked in the door and were met by the owner of the cutest restaurant. Gwen may be small in stature, but she has the biggest personality, and you can't help but love her the second you meet her. She introduced herself to us and gave us a big hug hello. The restaurant was filled with her grandbabies, and customers, and she had a lovely choice of homemade fried chicken, fish, mashed potatoes, gravy, and the best collard greens and broccoli cheese casserole I ever tasted. There was also a large choice of desserts and a beautiful salad bar, and more choices than I can name on her buffet, beautifully laid out. We enjoyed our visit at the restaurant so much; we exchanged addresses before we left. Every once in a while, you can meet someone once and just know you will be friends for a long time.

The rain never came while we were in the restaurant, at least nothing more than the sprinkle that had just started when we pulled off at the exit, but back on the interstate the roads were still soaked from the rain, letting us know we'd made the right choice.

Not very much later, we passed the Mississippi state line and stopped at the visitor's center. They are great places to stop and get ideas of what to see in the state. They had a beautiful display of sculptures made from the driftwood left from Hurricane Katrina. It is amazing how talented some people are. They were absolutely beautiful. While we were there, we checked TripAdvisor for a room in Biloxi, as my friend Alex said it was a fun place. We decided we deserved a play day, so we reserved the room for two days.

Riding into Biloxi, I instantly knew I was going to love this place. The left side of the road was lined with beaches along the Gulf of Mexico, and the right side of the street is hotels, motels, restaurants, casinos, and shops. It is an adorable beach town and I just happen to be a beach bum at heart.

After unloading the bikes, we decided to go celebrate Father's Day at one of the many casinos in Biloxi. We walked down the street about a mile and headed in to lose some money, and were 100% successful at it. On our walk home, we decided to try out a Waffle House as they are everywhere in the South and neither of us had ever been in one. Breakfast was good, and we continued back to our temporary home for the next two days, to get some sleep before we head out to discover more of Biloxi tomorrow.

Day Twenty – Biloxi, Mississippi
(6/19/17)

Today was a fun play day. We started at the beach and went shopping at a fun beachy shop on stilts, with a huge shark mouth which we had to grab a picture of us on the bikes in. It was clearly not made for driving through, but I just could not help myself. It just goes with playing tourist.

When we left the beach, we headed to the local Harley shop, because when we pulled into the motel last night I noticed the screw holding my handle bars on was almost completely out. Probably not a good thing to try and ride without handlebars, but I caught it before I was in trouble, so this was good. Being bikers, a trip to a new Harley shop is always something to look forward to. When we got to Mississippi Coast Harley Davidson, they were awesome. The mechanic came out and torqued the handle bars for me, and it turned out all four screws were loose. Of course, we couldn't stop and not buy something, so by the time we left I had a few new shirts, and Bonz had a new oil gage. Life is good!

My nephew Frank suggested going to The Shack, BBQ and Blues, so even though it was not raining, we decided it was a good time to eat. The place was awesome! It was like a mini city of shacks all set up around the restaurant. You could eat outside or inside. The bar was made from an old trucking container. We enjoyed checking the place out for a while before we headed inside to eat. Not only was the place very different, but the food was also very good. Thanks, Frank! I love unique places like this.

I guess there is an air force base very close by. A plane was landing, and I do believe I could have touched it from the parking lot of the motel. This was not a small two-engine plane; it was more along the same size as a jetliner! Totally freaked me out as I thought it was crashing in the backyard, until a guy explained that it was only landing at the base. This thing was not only huge, but very loud too. It definitely could wake the dead.

I made the mistake of not checking the weather past today when we got here. This area is expecting some tropical storms that are supposed to last a few days. When I checked the weather apps on my phone, they said 100% chance of thunderstorms for most of the day and night tomorrow. So it looks like we are staying another day or two. This town is so cute, and there are lots of new things to discover, so life could be much worse. We might even try losing some more money at the casino, since I am so good at that, but we will see.

Day Twenty-One – Biloxi, Mississippi
(6/20/17)

Well, we finally got caught in the middle of a rainstorm. Tropical thunderstorms for the next few days, with a possible hurricane in Louisiana. I am checking the weather to see if we can find a window to get out, but it is not looking good so far. I have ridden through thunderstorms before and they are no fun, and very unsafe. Most people in a car don't see you on the bike until they are right up on your tail, and whoever makes windshield wipers that work on a helmet will probably make a million dollars, as it is very hard to see out of the visor of the helmet in the rain. And rain just plain hurts at 70 mph. So I think we are going to have to bunker down and get some reading done. This is one advantage to not having to be anywhere for the next three weeks. Hopefully, the tropical storm will lose some of its thunder and start moving east instead of west, but I have no control over the weather, so we might as well make the best of it. At least we are not stuck in a tent!

We put on our rain gear and grabbed the umbrellas we brought for some shade in the desert, and walked down the road to find some place to eat. What an awesome badass look, NOT! At least no one knows us around here, so I didn't really care. We had a great meal at The Reef, with appetizers, dinner, and dessert, so life is looking up already. With this amount of water coming down, we are better off safe than sorry.

Well, the rains came in full force, and it was impossible to sleep as both phones kept going off with thunderstorm and tornado warnings. I went outside about 2:00 a.m. and the sky was the most beautiful dark burgundy and black color I have ever seen. I tried to get a picture of it, but it would not pick up the color correctly. All I could think of was the old rhyme, *Red sky at night, sailors' delight. Red sky at morning, sailors take warning*. The rhyme has been a rule of thumb used for weather forecasting during the past two millennia. It is based on the reddish glow of the morning or evening sky, caused by haze or clouds related to storms in the region. I do not think any sailors would be happy with a burgundy sky, though.

Day Twenty-Two – Biloxi, Mississippi
(6/21/17)

Well, we got out for a little while today. We walked across the street to check out the beach after the storm last night. The waves obviously were all the way up to the sand dunes, and the water was higher than an average high tide. The sky was still very angry, and there was no doubt that the lack of rain was going to be short-lived, but we found a beach chair that was not buried in the sand and hung out for a while, watching Mother Nature smolder before she showed her wrath again. The sky was so dark it felt like dusk, but it definitely had its own beauty. The torrents of water coming from the sky and ocean left beautiful etchings in the sand, and the lack of people on the beach allowed us to enjoy all this beauty left just for us. The one odd thing we did notice was there were no seashells on the beach, leaving the sand with an exceedingly clean look as the waves beat the shore.

It was obvious that the lack of rain was not going to last so, when it's raining, it must be time to eat! So we headed to Shaggy's Restaurant down the road and had a lovely meal. Bonz had a fried Cajon chicken thigh with homemade coleslaw that was about the size of a small chicken. I had a fish sandwich with French fries that was very tasty. Shaggy's has a lot of personality, with the storm windows open to allow the beautiful (and wet) breeze to pass through the restaurant, and all the beach paraphernalia hanging on the walls. Service was perfect and the skies opened up as we expected right after we entered.

It did not look like Mother Nature was even close to being done with her wrath, so we had a very wet walk back to the room. It made me realize how lucky we are to have the time to wait the storm out, instead of having to head out rain or shine. Most of our bike trips are much shorter, so the luxury of time on a horrible day is not usually an option. Like the time Tracy and I rode to Westchester, NY, for my high school reunion; it thunderstormed for the entire trip. I think it took my chaps a week to dry out when we got back. Or the time we went with Dave and Michelle to Bike Week in Sandusky, Ohio, not only through a thunderstorm that would not quit until the last 40 miles of the trip, but it was also so very cold that it took days to get the chill out of our bones.

This trip is not a trip of how far we can go and how fast we can get there. This trip is just about exploring these United States in all its glory. And if we don't take the time to smell the roses, we would miss what we came out to see. By the time we got back to the room, our phones were going off with another tornado warning. When Bonz turned on the weather, they were showing a tornado in the Gulf in the area we were the other day. Luckily, the Shack was not directly on the water, and hopefully it is safe through this storm, as we totally loved the place. There was also another tornado that hit the library at 8:30 this morning, just two miles down the road. So for now, we are going to sit back and enjoy being dry and warm, in our temporary home, and maybe see another awesome light show tonight as Mother Nature continues, until she calms down.

Day Twenty-Three – Biloxi, Mississippi
(6/22/17)

We got up this morning and checked the weather apps and it was still not looking good, so we headed to the office of the motel for our morning coffee and daily re-up on the room. I was hoping for a decent window to start heading west today but it was still not looking good. So while drinking our coffee and watching the lounge chairs take a dip in the pool through the rain and winds, we had a nice conversation with the motel manager. He brought out a photo album of all the damage from Hurricane Katrina that happened to the motel. Half the roof was missing on the back half of the motel and the whole front half of the motel was completely missing. The only thing still standing was the sign out front. With as beautiful as this area is, it is hard to believe that everything here was completely destroyed in 2005.

As we walked to the Casino the other day, we did notice a lot of empty lots covered by grasses that used to be parking lots. These lots obviously used to be attached to buildings that no longer exist. The motel manager explained that many people have left instead of rebuilding, in spite of the majesty of this area. I guess they learned first-hand that the power of Mother Nature should never be underestimated.

When we got back to the room, Bonz decided to take a nap. For some reason, he still thinks I snore, and blames his lack of sleep on this fictitious fact (as I have never heard myself snore). So when he got up from his nap, the rain had stopped. The skies were still pretty black, but the rain had stopped! We decided to go to the Biloxi visitor's center, as our neighbor had suggested this after his visit yesterday. The visitor's center was too far to walk, so we actually took the bikes. This was the first time we had even started the bikes since the storm started, and I was very happy to find that both bikes still started and my radio still worked. It was my little piece of freedom for the day.

We headed down the street towards the visitor's center and stopped at the Hard Rock Café and Casino, as it was definitely time to eat. By the time we ordered our burgers, the sky opened up again and the wind came back with a vengeance. So since we were also in a casino, we decided to make our contribution to the local economy by losing more money at The Hard Rock Casino. After we successfully lost our allotment to the casino, it looked like the rain had temporarily stopped again and we decided that now was a good time to try to ride home, and we lost that bet too.

Just as we turned out of the parking garage onto the road, the rain and wind decided to do another dance on us. Within about ten seconds, my goggles were so covered in raindrops that it was almost impossible to see out of them and between the sand, the puddling on the road, and the winds, my bike was just ice skating down the road in a lovely zig zag. Needless to say, we never made it to the visitor's center. I have decided that riding a motorcycle during a tornado and flashflood warning is probably not in my best interest, but it sure as hell beats looking at the four walls of this motel room. Hopefully tomorrow will allow us to start moving west to our next adventure. There is still hope.

Day Twenty-Four – Jennings, Louisiana
(6/23/17)

It finally stopped raining! I had been checking the weather apps and found a window, but it was a very early window. Anyone that knows me knows I am not a morning person. But after looking at the same walls for so many days, and having tried all the restaurants within walking distance, it was definitely time to hit the road again. I never thought I would miss the interstate as badly as I did. We were up at 6:00 am, and locked and loaded by 7:30. We made our window. It really turned out to be a great day for riding, way too hot for anything else.

We did all this with no coffee! First cup wasn't till we stopped at The Waffle House at 11:00 a.m. We missed most of the rain, only having to pull off once for a sweet tea break while the thunderstorm rolled by around 1:00. Other than that, we hit a few light showers but their cooling wetness was short-lived and extremely refreshing in the heat of the day.

It seems that most of the I-10 through Louisiana is just one huge bridge. Several major sections of the highway are elevated in Louisiana around the bayous and Lake Pontchartrain. I have never before seen bridges so long. They run above the swampland and interconnect (it feels) through the whole state. Because it is an interstate, it was not built for the views, but for convenience of getting where you need to go.

We decided to quit for the day when we hit Jennings, Louisiana. This little "town" is basically a huge truck stop. There are restaurants, motels, gas stations, a tiny casino (which we did not donate to this time), and a Wally World (Walmart) across the street. We checked online and the nearest nice

Cajun restaurant was 10 miles down Route 10, which we had just gotten off, and that was not happening.

My brother-in-law had suggested having shrimp étouffée, so we went in search of it, as we don't expect to be in Louisiana very long. We found it at a weird little restaurant inside a gas station convenience store, with a casino attached to it. A very small casino attached to it. Eating a seafood dish in this weird little restaurant did not look like the greatest of ideas, and even the salad dressing came in its own individual packaging, but it actually was quite good! Bonz had fried shrimp with a side of étouffée, no rice. They did not have the actual dish served with shrimp, so I tried it with crawfish, as that was the only choice. Who would have ever thought that all those crawdads we used to catch from the creek behind our house in Buffalo had the ability to taste so good! (Not really sure they are the same things I was eating, but that is all I could think of while doing so). See Russ, I lied. I did try the crawfish.

So now we are tired and full, so I'm signing off to hit the hay.

Assessing changes in our first quarter on the road:
Observations and speculations: (day 1-24)

So far we have made it through eight states, two time zones, and a bad case of bronchitis. My first look at the ocean made me realize just how far we had traveled. Our house is about eleven miles from Lake Ontario and Sandusky is right on Lake Erie. So we have successfully traveled from top to bottom of the US. This is a little empowering, as neither of us has ever ridden this far before. At first Bonz was a little apprehensive about taking the lead, and was stressing a little bit about how to get where we wanted to go. But we found what works for us, and I keep reminding him we can't get lost if we have no idea where we are going.

The GPS is on my bike and we have found that with the headsets it is easier, and safer, to have me read the GPS while he keeps an eye on the traffic around us. The funny thing is that I can only read the top left-hand corner of the GPS in the sunlight. The names of the streets and routes are washed out in the bright light. So the directions are always "in 2 miles we will take a right" or "in 1.5 miles we will bear left". So with no idea of what route we are really looking for, and guessing most of our turns, we are pretty successful at getting where we want to go without getting lost, and very few times do we have to make a U-turn.

As the days roll by, we are getting more comfortable with our setup and with listening to each other. We each have picked up different responsibilities and naturally work very well together. Our attitude is much more relaxed than it is when we are home and focused on things that need doing. It is funny how even a day at the laundromat can be fun on vacation. Letting go of the stress that consumes our everyday life has changed our attitudes to focus more on fun and less on what could go wrong on our trip. In the mornings we discuss where we are heading that day and whether we want to stay and play or head back out on the road to find new discoveries. In a world of "have to's," it does take some time to get used to all "want to's". Sometimes even good change takes some work.

I know most people do not like to talk about money, but I have no issues with this. It is a necessary evil, and I find stress levels go up as the bank account goes down. We have a very lucrative budget for this trip. Basically, we broke the bank and do not really plan on coming home with much. Budgeting and cutting back is a large part of our life at home; I did not want to have these worries on our trip. Just to give you an idea of our expenses, so far we have spent approximately $2000 on lodging, $1000 on food, and about $300 on gas. Of course, we have also spent $1000 more on incidentals. So our total for this quarter is about $4300. I only add this because it was a question I had when we were trying to prepare for our trip. There are many ways to cut back on spending if your budget is smaller, but we did not really worry about that for this trip. I am sure our next trip will not have such a lucrative budget, but we will tackle that when we get to it.

I think the only thing I would have changed so far would be to pack lighter when we left, and to test the weight distribution on the bike out locally before we were locked and loaded and headed out for the trip. Had I practiced using the tie-down method, it would have saved us a lot of time. But new things always need a learning curve.

Day Twenty-Five – Houston, Texas
(6/24/17)

We woke up in our motel this morning and there was water everywhere. There was a nice puddle next to the bathtub though we had not showered yet, and the wood floor was covered in a film of sweat. I have no idea where the water was coming from, but we were pretty happy to pack up and hit the road again. The weather apps were not looking good and, gladly, they were wrong again. It was another rough day full of interstate riding, to get away from the rains that are the after effect of Tropical Storm Cindy.

I really wish people would look before they try to move into a lane that we currently are occupying. The helmet communication we have has helped a lot when spotting idiot drivers. Luckily, there were no collisions. We hit I-10 and, about 20 minutes later, got caught in a thunderstorm that completely soaked us, but it was quite short-lived, and being that it was time to eat, we lucked out another totally different place for lunch. Basically, it was a meat market that also cooked food to eat in their dining area.

We met a few couples that gave us great ideas as to what to see in Texas, which was awesome, as I did not really plot out a lot on our trip for Texas. The weather was already in the nineties, and the weatherman said that it felt like 110 degrees, which he was not wrong about. The soaking felt wonderful, except inside. I find the only time you need a coat in the south is when you walk inside. It seems everyone has air conditioners that are definitely run on steroids.

We hit the Texas border, and my new thing is to stop at the welcome centers. I never used to stop, but I am finding them very interesting and full of cool information. And most have free coffee! If you ever pass a welcome center when traveling, I highly suggest stopping; you never know what you may learn. The welcome center for Texas did not have free coffee but they did have maps and lots of cool places to see. You could spend a month in this state and not see everything. Like the song says, "From the mountains, to the prairies, to the oceans white with foam …", Yes Texas has it all.

Now, riding the I-10 in Texas is kind of boring. The roads are pretty straight, except for all the construction going on. So to keep myself occupied, I started playing with the little gear looking thing at the top of my throttle. Well, it turns out after riding 2700 miles on this trip; I discovered that I have cruise control! What a girl I am, and what a relief to my aching right hand this wonderful discovery was. When we stopped the next time, we checked Bonz's bike and he has it too! Tomorrow is going to be a great day!

We decided to get the heck off I-10 in Houston and got a little turned around with the directions off my phone. So we pulled into a gas station to get an idea of where we were actually supposed to be going and immediately met two gentlemen that introduced themselves as fellow travelers and rail riders. Since one of the gentlemen was from Sodus, NY, we had to buy them a beer before we left. (It's a karma thing).

A little while later, we ended up taking another wrong turn (which is very easy in downtown Houston) and ended up in the parking lot of a Harley Davidson dealer. Well, this just meant it must be time to shop. I am a firm believer in following the signs, especially if they say Harley Davidson! They were out of pins with their name on them, so we picked up a poker chip and decided we were done for the day. We met a nice gentleman who was heading into the dealership (because all people are nice that shop at Harley Dealerships) and he gave us directions to a few hotels right around the corner.

We are staying at a Holiday Inn Express and it is 100% better than our last temporary home. Rita, who was working the desk, was so very friendly and helpful. It is people like her that really make a stay in a temporary home so wonderful. They even have Guest Laundry, which is very important as I have been wearing my jeans longer than I would like.

Day Twenty-Six – Houston, Texas
(6/25/17)

Today was a fun play day. Since we are in Houston, we decided that we would go check out a museum. So we went and got lost in the city again trying to find the National Museum of Funeral History. It is the only Funeral Museum in the USA. It is quaint, and quite full. There was a little glass snow-white coffin, and a coffin built for three. This was special ordered for two parents that had lost their child. The parents changed their mind on the suicide pact they had originally planned when ordering this special-made coffin, and it was never used. They even had baskets that they used to carry the fatally wounded soldiers in, this being where the saying a "basket case" came from. There was also a Batmobile there, in honor of Adam West's recent death. For such a small museum, there was a lot of really interesting stuff. If you're ever in Houston, I would highly recommend a trip to the National Museum of Funeral History.

Having been a part of the Elmwood Cemetery Association for the last 15 years or more, I do find graveyards and things associated with funerals a little fascinating. The Elmwood Cemetery is a small graveyard, run for the last 150 years by the people that live on the street. As Russ put it the first time he invited me to the meeting, they serve homemade cookies and are a great way to meet your neighbors, and both are true. There is so much local history to be learned in your local cemetery. The changing customs, and reasons traditions change, are also interesting. Did you know that cemeteries used to also be used as park areas? If you have an interest in local history, no matter where you live, I would suggest taking a trip to your local cemetery.

We stopped at a deli on our way back to the hotel and had a very nice dinner. Bonz jokingly reminded me that I did not get a picture of him eating this time, as I have been posting shots on Facebook of all his meals. The comments have been very funny, so I just have to apologize for missing posting one of his meals, and understand that I am not starving him today.

Day Twenty-Seven – Fredericksburg, Texas
(6/26/17)

The plan for today was to make it to San Antonio. The thought of getting back on I-10 to get there was not a fun thought. Dawn, my sister Karen's friend, had very graciously offered us a place to stay while in San Antonio, and gave us quite a few great places to ride to. I had to turn her down, as I just could not get back on I-10 again. We decided to head north and then west to see if we could find a nicer road. The problem with the interstate, other than all the trucks, is that you are missing the beauty of the state.

One of the suggestions Dawn had given us was Luckenbach, so we set the Garmin for Luckenbach and headed out to find better roads, and it worked! We were still on two-lane highways, but they cut through a few cute towns and passed many ranches. What is with all the albino cattle in Texas? We passed a few ranches that were covered with white cows; very odd. It was a much better day on the bikes than the past few have been. We stayed rain-free until about 30 miles from Luckenbach.

We pulled into a rest stop as the rain was getting harder, and Bonz hit clay. If you have ever done pottery, you would understand how slippery clay is when you add water. He started to make a right- hand turn and halfway into the turn his bike decided it wanted to fishtail down the hill onto the grass. The only safe way to get the bike to stop fishtailing and back onto the pavement was to continue on the grass past the fence, and around back to the road, before backtracking into the rest area. I was quite proud of how he kept the bike upright through the whole ordeal; he also scared the living shit out of me! He promised not to do that again, and leave the skateboarding tricks to the kids that actually do them on skateboards. But our son Josh would have been proud to see Dad do an Olly on his motorcycle. Sorry you missed it; it was a once in a lifetime thing.

We made it to Luckenbach just as the rain stopped. The place is awesome! It has a bunch of old buildings and a post office/general store and a few bars. Being that it was Monday, only the main bar was open. There was a food truck, if you were hungry, and Bonz is always up for a good meal. The food was really good, and we took it over to the picnic tables and watched the show.

Luckenbach is all about the music. They have music seven days a week. While we were there, multiple people got up to sing, and they even had a cowboy poet reciting his poems between songs. It was so much fun, we stayed for a while to watch the show. This place is another one for your bucket list of must- sees. On the way in, I saw a sign for camping and went into the post office to inquire about a site, but they only rented to RVs and no tent camping was allowed. So we rode to Fredericksburg and rented a room, which was probably a blessing as it is thunder and lightning, along with a downpour, as I write this.

Day Twenty-Eight – San Angelo, Texas
(6/27/17)

We woke up in Fredericksburg, Texas. This is a German town. There are many restaurants and little boutiques. It is actually quite large for a town, meaning there is more to it than just Main Street. The motel we stayed in last night was a cute older motel that looked more like multiple cottages all stuck together. It was over 60 years old, which showed its age by its lack of electrical outlets. Hey, I'm still a geek, and everything needs re-charging. They are slowly upgrading the rooms, which was obvious by the flat screen TV mounted to the wall.

The mass of wires could have been hidden better, and the TV re-booted every 5 minutes, and took about a minute to come back so any shows we were watching were a little hard to follow, but the room was very cute, like you would find at your sweet, adorable great-grandmother's house. The woman who ran the motel was very sweet too. All I could think of was, I would have so much fun re-doing all those rooms. I guess this train of thought comes from fixing up our old house for the last fifteen years. Some habits are hard to change.

After we were locked and loaded (bikes packed and tied down), we headed to town for some breakfast. The first four restaurants we tried were closed. It was too late for breakfast, and too early for lunch. We finally found one that was serving and had a nice soup and salad, and Bonz had a ruben with hot German potato salad for breakfast. On our way back to the bikes, we also got a little shopping done as the boutique would ship the goods home for me. Life is good.

We set the Garmin to San Angelo and headed out. The weather was perfect. The roads were perfect. The day was perfect. We rode down two- and four-lane highways that we had all to ourselves. We saw a car maybe once every half hour, if that. We now have the cruise control down, so I am learning to ride with my left hand, as I have never had that option before. We rode past multiple ranches. Everyone had an original ornate iron gate with their name on it, and every one of them looked locked. It made me wonder why. If I lived that far from my neighbors, I think I would love company.

Another thing I noticed is that Texas is covered with trees, but none of them are larger than a two-story house. Some of them are as wide as a house, just not very tall. They are awesome for shade and have branches like an apple tree, but thicker. They are the perfect tree to spend your time climbing, but at my age I would never have gotten down. There are also a ton of cacti growing all over the place here. I always thought of cacti growing in sand in the desert, but they are everywhere here. I am finding it very enjoyable to ride through Texas, and am a little humbled by the size of the ranches here, and the ability to see such expanse. It really is a very beautiful state, and if you're a biker, the empty roads are awesome!

We pulled into San Angelo in time for dinner. Got to feed the Bonz Man! I picked a restaurant on my Garmin that sounded like an authentic Texas restaurant, Rosa's Café. When we pulled in, we did notice a drive through, but it did not look like a chain restaurant and there were cars filling the parking lot, which is always a good sign. When we got in, you ordered your food at the counter and then went to sit in their adorable dining room. There were screens that let you know when your number was called, and the food was awesome! It was such a fun combination of a five-star Mexican restaurant and a fast food joint that was very tastefully done. I was impressed.

Day Twenty-Nine – Big Springs, Texas
(6/28/17)

Okay, it was a hot one today, high nineties. We did not have that far to go today, so we decided to do a little tourist stop in San Angelo. I found a bordello museum in town, so after breakfast at the hotel, we packed up and headed into town. Miss Hattie's Bordello did not open until 2:00 p.m., so we went shopping. There were a bunch of little boutiques that all connect to the bordello, or did when it was still in use, so we browsed for a while. One of the boutiques had a small basket filled with green and pink plastic army men. The sign said to take one and place it somewhere you would see it often, so you can pray for our soldiers. I thought that was a really neat idea. So I took a pink one.

We were done shopping at noon and as we just finished eating, we decided not to hang around till 2:00 for the tour. It would have been fun, but hitting the road at 3:00 was a little late. Maybe next time we are here we will get to see the museum.

There were a few more cars on our private four-lane highway today, but not enough to bother anyone. You can ride for quite a few miles before you see a small town, or anything at this point, in Texas. We saw a lot of trees that were no bigger than a two-story house, and many fences, but not many entrances to ranches. I really like those. We did see a lot of windmills and a few pump jacks getting oil out of the ground. That was pretty cool, and as they were running near the windmills, I also found that to be a little bit of an oxymoron. But since that land has been used up to get the oil out for years, I guess it is a perfect place for the windmills. The neighbors won't complain, as I saw very few houses spread out along the way.

Did I say it was hot? Wow, between the sun and the lack of shade, and the heat permeating off the blacktop, it was a very hot ride today. Add chaps and the degrees only go up, but my bike did not use me as a human ironing board, so all was good.

We decided to camp today, as the weather apps are not calling for rain. The first campground I called did not allow tent camping, but the second one did. There are a lot of RV parks in the area, because most are filled with the guys working on the pipeline. These people have to leave their families for a year or more to find work. We were talking with a nice couple and their young daughter; she took the summer off to see her husband, and he has been living here for over a year, in an RV.

I asked about the winters and he said it does get very cold (it will go below zero) but there's not much snow. I always thought living in an RV would be a lot of fun, but in my dream world we would always be somewhere where the weather would be warm. I freeze in my camper in the spring and fall and cannot imagine having to live there in the winter, although there are some that I know that do. It really makes you take a look at how blessed we have really been. I would really miss my Bonz if he or I had to separate for work. Bad enough we worked separate shifts, but he always got up early to see me before I had to go in. There is so much that we don't hear about happening in these United States, until you actually talk to the people living it.

Day Thirty – Lubbock, Texas
(6/29/17)

We had a lovely morning at the campsite. The weather dropped during the night, so sleeping was easy. We left the top of the tent off so we could enjoy the breeze. Absolutely no privacy, but in this heat, who cared? Bonz napped when we got there, so I hung the top of the tent from the tree and staked it in the ground and it made a perfect shaded area for reading before bed.

In the morning, a bunch of guys were cleaning out a large box trailer and came over and talked to Bonz, as they were afraid of waking me up. I was sleeping in. He explained they didn't have to worry, as his wife can sleep through anything. When I finally got up around 8:00, we made coffee and oatmeal for breakfast and met a really nice woman walking her dog. Her husband was also working the pipeline. He retired, and decided to make a career change, and now they travel all over working on the pipe line. They had just left Ohio. She was also retired, so she could travel with him.

The advantage of the tent site being in the doggie area is we got to meet all the people with puppies. We were definitely an anomaly, as we were the only tenters in the park. We took our time packing up as we did not have very far to go today, and the coffee was plenty. We were locked and loaded by 11:00 a.m. and ready to hit the road. One of the guys working on the trailer came over and told us that Big Springs has the oldest Harley Davidson Dealer in Texas. Well, that sounded way too good to pass up, so off we went to buy a new pin.

The Harley Dealer was not far from the campsite. We went in and had a nice conversation with the owners. They have been a family-owned dealership since 1926, and it is still owned by the same family. It wasn't the largest dealership, but it was definitely well-loved. They'd just gotten new pins with a picture of the dealership in 1926 on it, and luckily they'd come in two days ago, so my timing was perfect! They gave us some great suggestions on where to eat in Lubbock and Amarillo, Texas. It always warms my heart when you meet really good people.

Did I say it was hot yesterday? Well, I lied. Today was HOT. We headed up 87, and rode right through all the oil wells pumping the oil from the ground. The farmers were planting crops all around the oil pumps, but as they were plowing you could see the dust billowing up into the wind. I'm not sure what you can grow on land that dry in this heat, but I am guessing it is hay for all the animals on the ranches.

The temperature hit 105 degrees. After riding for about 45 miles, we hit a small town and gassed up. There was no shade at the gas station, so we went across the street to a McDonald's, and ordered a snack and a very large drink. While we were enjoying the air conditioning, a nice gentleman came over with his son and we got the pleasure of his company for about an hour. He was working in the cotton field in 105 degrees. I can just not imagine. He also had traveled a lot in the west on his motorcycle, and also gave us many ideas of where to stop. The air was good; the company was good; and the drink was very large.

When we left, we started down the road about 20 feet, and I had to ask Bonz if it was raining, as I was getting very wet. We pulled over and realized I had a problem with the gas line. I looked online and the nearest Harley Dealer was 60 miles away. We do have triple A, but I don't think 60 miles is a free tow. While I was looking it up on my phone, Bonz spotted a service station next door and went and talked to the guy working there. He offered to look at it and had it running like new in no time. He was working on opening a shop to work with his son.

I think that is so cool; crafts are not as readily passed down from one generation to another, and when you see this, it is very heartwarming. They both loved to build race cars, and had a few at his shop he was working on. When all was said and done, he wanted to just charge us ten dollars for his time, when he had even left to go pick up the part we needed. So Bonz gave him forty, and thanked him again. He probably saved us hundreds in the tow alone. See? There are angels among us, and for this I will always be forever grateful.

By the time we hit the road again, it was after 4:00. This was not a very good time to be hanging out in the hot sun on a 105-degree day. The wind was even hotter than the sun. The ride was only 60 miles to Lubbock, but it felt like forever. We finally got to the hotel and jacked the air all the way up. It took a little while to cool down again so we could unpack the bikes. By that time, we were done for the day and ordered pizza to the room. So, sore and tired, I am headed to bed so we can get up and do it again, amen.

Day Thirty-One – Lubbock, Texas
(7/1/17)

Well, today I gave my lily-white ass a break. We went to the Buddy Holly Museum. I knew he died young but had never realized he was only twenty-two years old. It is kind of fascinating that that someone so young could make such huge changes in so many lives and only be on this earth for twenty-two years. They have restored his drummer's house, JI Alison, and another fascinating thing is his house has my kitchen cupboards in it and the exact same coffee table that is currently in my attic. And, the side table was very close to the one in my hallway with all the plants on it.

I remember going to the Strong Museum in Rochester, NY, with my mom, and her finding things she grew up with in them and her thinking she was getting old. That was my reaction to seeing this museum; I am definitely getting old. I used to call myself a classic, but over 50 (if you're a car) is no longer a classic. Now I guess I am just another museum piece, because I refuse to call myself an antique yet.

After the museum, we went to JJ&J's steakhouse, because the gentleman we met at McDonald's recommended it. He was right; the food was awesome. We could not ride all the way through Texas and not have a steak. That would have been sacrilegious.

When we got back to the room, Bonz took a nap and I went out and enjoyed the indoor pool. I enjoyed not baking in the sun, as I am a very well-done piece of meat at this moment, and read my book. Not a bad day for a day off.

Day Thirty-Two – Amarillo, Texas
(7/1/17)

Well, it is official. Our vacation is one-third over. We expected to be farther along, but ran into way too many cool things to stop at. I don't think three months is enough time to see all that is cool in the US, but it is a good start. I thought I might be homesick by now, but I think we are getting the rhythm down. When I read books on traveling through the south on a motorcycle, they usually do it in the fall. I think it may be because the rain and tornado season is during June.

But we did pretty good at hitting most of our original planned stops, considering we were basing most of our trip on the weather. We did get a little wet, but we have gone on weekend trips through much worse weather. We did miss New Orleans, because of Tropical Storm Cindy, but we had the unexpected pleasure of discovering Biloxi, Louisiana. I do so love that place. So it was a fair trade off. We also got to play in the Smoky Mountains, and that is definitely a do-over. I have never seen such beautiful country that was so motorcycle friendly. And we made a few friends I still keep in touch with. If you like to ride, the Smoky Mountains is a must see.

Another of my favorites was Luckenbach, Texas. If you're into a nice relaxing musical experience, this is definitely a must-see, and if you're musically inclined, please bring your instrument. If I ever get back to Texas, I would love to spend more time in the San Antonio area as there were more sites to see than we had time for. But that is okay, as I was running out of things for my bucket list.

Last night we got a taste of a Texas thunderstorm. We saw it coming, as there was a huge marshmallow cloud in the sky, and it was having its own light show. I have never seen lightning stay within a cloud like that before. It was more like fireworks and less like lightning, because I never saw it touch the ground. I thought it was going miss us as when we were watching it, the huge cloud looked miles away, but later that night the rain came in torrents and the thunder was so loud, it shook the building. I absolutely love thunderstorms (when I am not on my motorcycle) and this one was awesome.

When we got up in the morning, the rains had cooled everything down, and the roads were still wet, so it must have dumped a lot of rain. So it made for a perfect day to ride! The fields had more green in them than I have seen in Texas yet, and no clouds of dust that we were seeing a few days ago. Being that it is now the Fourth of July weekend, we did have more traffic join us on our own personal road (Route 27), but I would not call the road crowded at all, by upstate NY standards. The landscape to Amarillo is pretty flat, allowing us to see the enormous vastness of Texas. I have never seen farms as extensive as they are here. There is a complete calmness, very Zen like, that comes over you as you ride through farmlands. So todays' ride would be ranked a ten out of ten.

We made it to Amarillo and had to go to the Big Texan Steak Ranch. This place is on Route 66 and will give you your meal for free if you can eat a salad, three shrimp, a baked potato, and a seventy-two-ounce steak within an hour. The people we met at the oldest Harley Dealership in Texas, and the gentleman we met in McDonald's, both recommended a stop there, so it was our first stop in Amarillo. If you want to find really cool places, just ask the locals; they know where all the treasures are hidden.

After we ate an awesome meal, we spent some time looking around, as there is so much to see there. In the back was an outdoor bar that was not being used at the time, as it was too early. They had a stage set up for a one-man band, and what looked like a gate that opened up for larger bands. They had a little jail and a stagecoach, and a cute game where they had different plaques with a hook, and a large ring tied to a string. The goal was to toss the ring onto the hook. It definitely looked easier than it was.

The whole bar area was set with a Wild West look and done very well. Inside the restaurant there was an outhouse and if you opened the door, there was an animated guy in there giving you grief, but was very funny. There was a large shooting range with seats made out of horse saddles, and a beautifully set up Wild West set to shoot at. When you walked outside, there was a motel next door that was designed to look like an old western town. This was also very well done, and not cheesy at all. I would have loved to see the inside of the rooms, but that was not an option.

Since we are now officially on Route 66, we decided to get a cheap motel room, as it is definitely in keeping with the Route 66 ambiance. Our cheap motel turned out nicer than quite a few other places that we have stayed, so that was definitely a bonus. All in all, today was a very good day.

Day Thirty-Three – Tucumcari, New Mexico
(7/2/17)

I was a little slow moving this morning, as there was no coffee at the motel. My main addiction in life is coffee. Without it, I have trouble breathing, let alone walking. So packing up and tying down the bikes did not go quickly. So our first stop was a cute little donut shop down the road. It was a small family-owned place that the locals come to so they can visit with each other. We met a few people there and stayed longer than originally planned, enjoying the company of the other patrons and the wonderful freshly made donuts and fresh brewed coffee.

One of the patrons was going to NY this summer to visit his sister. And the couple we talked to gave us a few new ideas of places to stop along our way. We have seen really great places by talking to people along the way; things like tips on where to stop are always accepted as beautiful gifts. We have been very lucky on our trip, and met some wonderful people along the way.

After my allotted gallon of coffee, one of the gentlemen staying at the motel suggested heading down to Georgia Street, between Avenues One and Six, and said it is where all the bikers go. So off we went. It was a cute part of town filled with restaurants and bars that cater to bikers. It looked pretty cool, but we had just finished breakfast and it was not raining, so we decided to head on down Route 66, which we were already on. So I set the GPS to the next attraction on our way.

We headed out to see the Cadillac Ranch. You cannot drive (or ride) Route 66 through Amarillo and not stop to see the Cadillac Ranch. It is ten Cadillacs buried so the ass ends are sticking out, and the art structure is in the middle of a field. The fun part is to bring your spray paint cans and graffiti the cars (which we did not do). They are covered in paint, and the cars and ground are all covered in many layers of graffiti. It is an Amarillo landmark, and has been mentioned in songs and used for rock and roll album covers over the years. We were not the only ones stopping. There were many other people there enjoying spray painting, and others just enjoying this anomaly.

Our next stop on Route 66 was the café that was featured in the Pixar/Disney movie *Cars*. We got to meet the woman that the car Flo was designed around, and The Midpoint Café was adorable, but not serving food at the time we stopped. Midpoint it is the halfway point between California and Chicago. She no longer owns the café, but runs a very cute gift shop next door. We stayed for a while and did some shopping and played tourist and took many pictures.

I absolutely love that movie, so stumbling on some of its origins was very fun. Like they say sometimes, the best stories are based on some facts. These are always fun to discover. She suggested stopping at the truck stop about three miles from the New Mexico line, and said the diner there had very good food. As I had not fed my Bonz much today, it was sounding like a very good suggestion.

Flo also explained that the old Route 66 does disappear at times and you have to get back on Route 40. Route 40 is an interstate with a speed limit of 75 MPH. Old Route 66 runs parallel to Route 40, about 15 feet from it, is also used as an access road, and has a 55 MPH speed limit, so it is rarely used. There is a reason that there are many windmills along this section of road, as it is always very windy; the winds were much easier to handle at a slower pace. So we decided we liked having our own road and, as no one else was using the old Route 66 road, headed off to New Mexico.

At the truck stop and tourist information center, we had a wonderful meal at a very reasonable price. They also had a free antique car museum, with a few old Harleys in it. So, after dinner, we decided to check this out. We ran into three guys on GoldWings pulling trailers. After tying up the bikes every day for the last month, the trailers looked really good. Of course, we had questions for them, and had a nice conversation before we headed back out to Route 66.

When we got to Tucumcari, after singing Little Feat's "Willing" most of the way, the town was pretty empty, while still being lined with motels. It was Sunday evening, and everything was closed. We found a cheap motel across from the only open restaurant and checked in. A friend of mine, Gordon, had suggested Tucumcari, and we had put that in as our destination.

It looks like a college town, as there are signs on some businesses that state students are welcome. Being that it is July already and school is closed might also be a part of why this town looked so desolate. We decided to head across the street to grab something to drink, and a snack, because the soda machine at the motel was not working, and hydration in high 90s is important.

When we walked in, we recognized Bill at the bar, so we joined him. He was one of the GoldWing riders that we had met earlier in the day, going from Biloxi to Durango, Colorado, for a weeks' vacation on the bike. He was enjoying a frozen Margarita, and it looked so good that I ordered a virgin strawberry daiquiri and Bonz ordered an NA Beer. The service was very slow, but the company was good, so we stayed for a while and enjoyed ourselves. The restaurant closed at 10:00 p.m., and we left a very short while before they closed. I could not figure out why I was so tired. Bonz reminded me we had passed another time zone, so it was actually midnight by NY time. This made me feel a little better as I crawled into bed for a good night's sleep, after a very fun play day.

Day Thirty-Four – Albuquerque, New Mexico
(7/3/17)

Well, this morning we woke up and walked across the street for coffee, so it already started out great! We cheated and left everything loaded on the bikes so we did not have to tie everything down, so this made it a fantastic morning! We headed out down Route 66 until it ended and then had to jump on Route 40 for about 70 miles. The traffic was a lot lighter and the weather was cooler (because we got an earlier start), so the ride was good.

We stopped in Santa Rosa at the Blue Hole (very original name). It is basically a pond in the middle of the desert that is 60 feet in diameter and 81 feet deep. The pond is fed from a natural underground vast system of water that connects the seven lakes. The water is crystal clear and the blue comes from the depth of the water. There are rocks surrounding the back of the hole, making it perfect for diving in, and is so deep people come from all over to scuba dive in the desert. Yep, you heard that right, scuba dive in the desert. (What an oxymoron.) As it was in the high 90s today, I removed my shoes and socks, rolled up my jeans, and waded in. It was very tempting to jump in, but the water was 61 degrees, and that may sound warm but it felt freezing. Wading in was enough to cool me down, as I really hate riding in wet clothes.

We stopped at a few other stops, but they were not very interesting. We passed about twenty billboards for the Circle A Ranch, so we stopped. I guess all stops can't be gems, because this one was not. It was a huge gift shop with a fast food place to eat. Definitely not my favorite stop, but that did not deter me from shopping. Hey, I was there.

At Moriarty, New Mexico, we got back on old Route 66 and had an awesome ride into Albuquerque. The landscape was just breathtaking as we rode up into the mountains. We passed another biker on the route that was also going slow, as he had his camera out and was filming the beauty. It is times like this that a Go-Pro would really be fun to have. But I am probably the only one that would enjoy watching an unedited clip like that. I remember the home movies my dad would have us sit and watch of a client's vacation that we did not even know (he was a salesman), when we were kids. I remember how painful those nights were, and could never make anyone else sit through that. This was back in the days when people came in from out of town for work, and the salesmen would bring them home to entertain them. That was their job. Ours was to act like the perfect family, with six kids. We were not always successful at our part. But Mom had this natural ability to make everything look normal and calm in the midst of all the crazy.

When we got settled at a motel that allowed dogs, we texted Connor and Chelsea the address, as they are driving back to Rochester, from California, and we made plans to meet up. It is so fun to see familiar faces after a month of not knowing anyone but Bonz. (My poor Bonz. And he still likes me!) So now I am heading to sleep, as we have new people to go out and discover with tomorrow!

Day Thirty-Five – Albuquerque, New Mexico
(7/4/17)

I love to read. But a good book is like crack to me, and I am much safer with a boring and slow-moving book. Needless to say, I stayed up till 5:30 and finished the book I was reading, which left me quite tired all day. If you want to lose a day or two, go ahead and read Bright Side, by Kim Holden, it will leave you in tears, with a smile on your face.

I woke up at 8:00 with my phone alarm and headed to the lobby for some coffee. Bonz was already enjoying his Java, and we stayed and allowed Connor and Chelsea to sleep. When everyone woke up, we headed over to Denny's for the big breakfast. Well-fed, we headed to the other side of town to take the tram up the mountain. It was very close to 100 degrees and the weather at the top of the mountain was 72. It was a fifteen-minute ride up the mountain in the tram, and very beautiful. If you're ever in the area, I would highly recommend this trip. There are multiple trails for mountain biking and hiking. When you get to the top, you can stay and take the tram down whenever you are ready, so no pressure, and I like no pressure. We were also enjoying the wonderful 72 degrees at the top.

As Connor and Chelsea are on a budget moving back to Rochester, NY and we have so rarely used the camping equipment, we offered to (actually more like begged) let them use the camping equipment on their travels. So I just lost another 50 lbs., while enjoying the ability to still eat as I like! I showed Connor how to use our weird little stove and helped him tie the bag on the top of the car. So Bonz is very happy about not having to camp anymore, as there are weird things like bears and snakes in the area, and I like the coffee served in the lobby.

When we got back to the motel, I took a nice nap as my eyes were rolling into the back of my head from lack of sleep. After a few hours, we ordered pizza and went outside to enjoy the fireworks.

They are legal here, so on the Fourth of July the entire city erupts in fireworks; these can be seen from anywhere outside. Having never lived in an area that fireworks are legal, this is a pleasant change. They have been going off for hours, and you never know where to look for the next explosion. It is kind of fun, and no traffic jams to see them.

This was a very fun day exploring with Connor and Chelsea. I am so glad we had this opportunity to connect as we both head in opposite directions in our travels across this great country.

Day Thirty-Six – Gallup, New Mexico
(7/5/17)

Well, today was our last play day on Historic Route 66. Connor and Chelsea headed out after our free breakfast at the motel. There was not really much to choose from, but I never used to eat breakfast, and now I look forward to my yogurt every day.

Packing up was easier because I was short the heaviest bag. What a difference that made! I am now realizing the issues I was having with the wind had a lot to do with the uneven weight of that huge bag. Today my bike was naked, and I totally enjoyed the ride. The Historic Route 66 kept weaving on and off Route 40. We took the Mother Road as often as we could. But it was still a lot of Route 40 (the interstate). The difference is that my bike handled the 55 mph winds we hit so much better. It was a lot more like riding on an Eagle than manhandling a bucking bronco, like it has been for the past 4000 miles.

I was no longer falling way behind, so the trucker with the demented sense of humor could no longer cut between us and then slow down, allowing all the other trucks to go ahead of him, behind

Bonz, like the one truck was doing the day before yesterday. (He did not think I noticed his little game, but I did.) Yep, not happening again. Life is good!

Our first stop was in Grants. We found a cute family-owned diner, and the waitress was just full of personality. This is one of the reasons that I love diners. I can't remember the name, but it is the purple building right off the exit. She told us how much she loves living in the area; it was quite infectious. It is a beautiful town surrounded by the beautiful New Mexico mountains. I don't know the correct name, but New Mexico mountains are all made from rocks and the tops are cut off each and every one of them. Some parts look like very large stepping stones. Totally breathtaking. After a great meal, we were back on old Route 66.

As we rode down Route 66, the sky was absolutely beautiful blue with white puffy clouds, except for one very large black cloud off to the left. Bonz does not like riding in thunderstorms, and I kept telling him nothing to worry about. Truth was, if it did storm there was absolutely no place to stop and find refuge from the storm; just us, the road, and the mountains. I absolutely love having my own personal road. We did hit a few teardrops while watching the rain pour down off to our left, but the storm totally missed us. That huge black cloud was a Godsend as it did grant us a lot of shade (which is rare in this area) for our ride today, keeping the temperature at a lower degree than most other days.

While we were meandering down our own personal road, we saw many billboards for Indian Village, and as the sky was still quite angry looking, I asked Bonz to stop. Inside there was a case of handmade jewelry that was just exquisite. All the pieces were handmade by different Navajo artists. So while Bonz sat outside worrying about the rain, I enjoyed myself shopping inside.

The last part of the ride was back on Route 40, so when we hit Gallup we exited at the first Gallup exit to figure out where we were actually going. While checking my TripAdvisor app, another biker came over to chat. He was traveling alone from South Carolina to California and looping like us up through South Dakota, and back home. We have met many bikers traveling alone on our trip, all men. It takes a lot of balls to take a trip like that by yourself, but many guys do it. I turned him onto the TripAdvisor app and showed him how we were using it and looked up the park he was asking about. He was also camping for his trip, but agreed carrying the extra weight was not worth it if you are not camping four out of seven days. After a nice chat, he headed off and I continued to search for a hotel.

Now, Bonz and I have been discussing paying to the Gods of Karma since we ran into our rail riding friends, and I bought them a few beers. We find if we do not help out the people that ask for money when we stop to gas up, something slightly bad happens, and when we do help out our fellow man, something slightly good happens. So a gentleman came over looking for liquor or money for a drink, and I was searching for a hotel and apologized as I had no cash on me. He thanked us and headed on to find someone a little more lucrative.

The motel we chose was about ten miles away on the other side of town, so we headed off to check in. When we got there, the line was about six deep, but the desk clerk assured us there was enough room for everyone. We checked into room 129, again five stars for giving us the first floor; this makes loading and unloading the bikes much easier. Before we unloaded the bikes, we went in and were enjoying the air conditioning and checking the news on the TV, when karma caught up again.

All of a sudden, the door opened up, and I thought the woman opening the door was going to have a heart attack when she saw Bonz lounging (fully clothed) on the bed. Turns out the motel double booked our room (which we just got 20 minutes ago). Turns out she was very nice and apologetic and went back to the desk to get an empty room. See? Karma is a real thing, and sometimes we need a subtle reminder.

Day Thirty-Seven – Winslow, Arizona
(7/6/17)

We woke up this morning and looked at a map. We don't have to be in Utah until the 11th, and it was only 371 miles away, so we have lots of play days left. The weather was nice, around upper 70s, so we decided to head to Sedona, Arizona. If we did that we could play on 66 for a few hundred miles. It sounded like such a good idea this morning. We found old Route 66 and it lasted for about ten miles. Of course, there was more shopping to do at Indian City before we got back on

40. We met a gentleman that lives on the reservation. He explained that the Navajo nation is the largest reservation in the States. He was out for a walk, which was very impressive in the heat considering it was many miles to the nearest house.

Route 40 runs through the reservation and it is very large. There is basically nowhere to stop on 40 and no shade anywhere. The weather just continued to climb. Finally, we saw a sign for a town, about 100 miles past Indian City. Of course, it was just the beginning of the hottest part of the day. The temperature got to a bubbling 105 degrees today, and my skin was on fire. I hadn't eaten all day, so stopping for a late lunch was in order. We found a Denny's and ordered a light lunch as it really was way too hot to eat much.

We decided to take a look at the map and find a place to quit for the day. We realized Winslow, Arizona, was just 30 miles from where we were, so decided this would be perfect. We headed out after lunch and rode into Winslow and rented a room. After walking into the air conditioning, we successfully took a nap till our body heat cooled down; we did not even unload the bikes. And that felt good.

A few hours later we headed down to Standing on the Corner Park, took lots of pictures and had a nice dinner, and headed back to the room to take a nap. Standing on the Corner Park is dedicated to the Eagles song "Take it Easy." It is a corner lot downtown with a mural of a girl in a flatbed Ford. There is also a restored Ford truck parked on the street, with two statues of the writers. It really was nicely done. People are constantly doing what we just did, pulling into town to take pictures of the corner.

The town is very cute, with a lot of little stores, but most were closed for the day, so after dinner we headed back to our temporary home for the night.

Day Thirty-Eight – Bellemont, Arizona
(7/7/17)

We are finally getting smarter. The weather has had a lot to do with what we've seen and what we have not gotten to visit. Last month it was running from the thunder and lightning storms, and now that we are in the desert, we are hiding from the sun and 100-plus degrees. This morning we woke up at 6:00 a.m., had breakfast (mostly coffee), and packed up and headed out by 8:00 a.m. The weather was absolutely beautiful. In the desert, the weather drops a lot at night; so early morning is just perfect to be out riding in the sun. We headed to Sedona, as our friend Gary and Sue have spoken so highly of the place, and their pictures were absolutely beautiful. They did not lie; the mountains are totally breathtaking. We got a little lost and took a beautiful ride through the mountains before we found Sedona and the beautiful mountains we saw in our friends pictures.

We stopped at the cutest café, Miley's Café, a favorite of the locals. Locals always know the good places to stop. As the temperature was quickly climbing, we had a nice light lunch. Everything was perfect, and the restaurant was designed adorably. If you're in the area, I highly recommend this café for a bite to eat.

Next door was the most delightful boutique, Bilby and Moss. We enjoyed a nice conversation with the owner and, of course, I had to shop. This time it was for Bonz. He has been looking for a bracelet, and we found the most unique bracelet I have ever seen. This day and age, unique is very difficult to find.

The weather was quickly climbing and it was over 100 degrees by the time we finished lunch, so we headed back towards Flagstaff. We would have stayed longer, but my lily-white skin has a bit of an issue in temperatures over 100 degrees; it does not bother Bonz as much. I think this could be because for the last twenty-seven years his job as a die caster had temperatures of 120 degrees every summer. Luckily, the temperature quickly dropped as we headed up the mountain. The difference in temperature was such a blessing.

We decided since we had some extra time, we should stop at the nearest Harley Davidson dealer and replace our tires and get an oil change. They were very helpful and nice there. They made time to do the oil changes today, even though they were very busy, but they had to order the tires, so we are going to drop the bikes off at 11:00 tomorrow. We found a motel about half a mile from the shop, so we can walk back after dropping off the bikes.

We have spent the last three days riding along the Navajo reservation. The reservation is 27,413 square miles, and is the largest reservation in the United States. They also helped us win WWII by using their language to communicate (also known as Code Talkers), and this language could not be broken/understood by the Germans, giving us the edge of encrypted communication during the war. Did you know the Navajo Indians were the first to tell mother-in-law jokes? They have also successfully lived off some of the most beautiful and barren land I have ever seen. They have left the land as it originally was, and for this glorious gift, they have paid dearly. The reservation does not allow any alcohol. But, of course, there are bootleggers that still sell liquor on the reservation at a large profit, and towns like Gallup, with their three liquor stores and bars catering to the Native American.

The issue is very obvious. Alcoholism goes hand in hand with poverty, and this breaks my heart. Living in recovery myself for the last nineteen years, I know personally that there is a better way. I also know recovery is not for people who need it; it only works for people who want it. This horrible disease has ruined more lives in the US. It is just sad to see its mark on the reservation also.

Day Thirty-Nine – Bellemont, Arizona
(7/8/17)

Well, not much to write about today. We got up late and brought the bikes back to Grand Canyon Harley Davidson to get the tires put on. The hotel is right across the Route 40 bridge, about three quarters of a mile away. We walked back to the motel and were going to read, but I successfully took a long nap instead. After a call from the dealership, we walked back to pick the bikes up. I almost did not recognize my bike. It was sparkling clean! We have been too busy having fun to wash them for the last 4000 miles, so they were in pretty filthy shape when we dropped them off. They checked the brakes and all was good, so just new tires and oil changes were all we needed. They also adjusted the foot pegs on my bike because they were real loose, and turned in an uncomfortable position; not anymore! We were both very happy with the service and very grateful that they squeezed us in. Five stars in our book!

Right next door was a bar, The 66 Roadhouse Grill. We went in to grab a bite to eat before we headed back to the room. It was a pretty cool biker bar. You ordered the meat you want and cooked it yourself. Pretty awesome! Especially since I have my own personal grill master with me! Bonz got a big old hunk of sirloin and I had a hot dog. They had a pretty good salad bar that went with the meal, so all is good in our world. We hung out for a while and met a guy from Flagstaff. He loves living in this area.

Considering we are in Arizona, the weather is so much nicer here. (We are about 10 miles out of Flagstaff). We are in the mountains, so when it was 110 degrees in Sedona and the reservation, it was only in the lower 90s here. This is another motorcycle friendly area, with many great roads to run for a daytrip. He is a truck driver and gave us good places to stop on our way to Utah. We are near the Grand Canyon, so most hotels are running at 100 to 500 dollars a night and get more expensive as we get closer to the Canyon. As it is threatening rain all day, Bonz is still happy we have no camping gear, so I can't make him camp in the rain. All in all, it was another great day.

Day Forty – Page, Arizona
(7/9/17)

We woke up early this morning and were showered and locked and loaded by 8:00 a.m. The weather in the desert is not too bad in the mornings. We headed back to Flagstaff and grabbed I-89 north. What a beautiful road. We came down off the mountain and back through the reservation. As I am learning, the weather is always hotter on the reservation land. Along the road are small shacks that native artists sell their wares from, pottery, beautiful handmade blankets, and lots of jewelry. Of course, I had to stop.

We also had the pleasure of riding past and through the Grand Canyon. It is funny how you can ride a few miles and watch the terrain gradually change. The beautiful painted mountains that we had the pleasure to ride past and through were totally breathtaking. We stopped at a lookout on top of a mountain and got to see a bird's eye view of the Canyon. The mercury was climbing on the thermometer, so we did not go into the park, but kept riding up to Page where we had a reservation for the night.

This being summer, and also being so close to the Grand Canyon, finding a place to stay was a little more difficult than usual. When I went on TripAdvisor this morning, the hotel I was originally trying to get was sold out during the time it took me to insert my credit card number, so this was the first time I actually made a reservation before we were ready to quit for the day, as we were warned it might be difficult if I made it this morning, before we left.

Page, Arizona, is a strange little town in the middle of nowhere. After riding the old Route 66 and seeing how an interstate can totally crush so many small towns, and looking at the poverty left behind, Page is the exact opposite. This town definitely caters to the rich. It is filled with hotels and fast food restaurants. But I did not notice any housing developments, and there are no trees to hide one. It is a town created for tourists. Actually, it is a town in the middle of nowhere that caters to rich tourists.

We are in the middle of the desert and there is a golf course across the street with green grass and sprinklers to keep it that way. There is even a Walmart here, so there are no small locally-owned shops or boutiques, which I have come to expect in small towns that cater to the rich. I find the contrast so very weird. So much poverty everywhere, except in Page, Arizona. I assume this is because of the proximity to the North Rim of the Grand Canyon.

So when in Rome, do as the Romans do ... So I grabbed my book and hung out at the pool. Being that they cater to the rich, the water was perfectly clean and very warm. The water temp could be an after effect of the 100-plus degrees it has been in Arizona lately, but I will take the good when I can find it.

Day Forty-One – Hurricane, Utah
(7/10/17)

Have you ever woken up in the morning not expecting much from a day, and then had your mind blown? That was today. I thought the beauty of the topless mountains we saw yesterday near the Grand Canyon was stunning. As we had already passed the Canyon, I did not expect much as we headed north to Utah, but I was so very wrong. From the minute we passed the Welcome to Utah sign, our surroundings just kept getting better. Not only was it the coolest day this week, not even breaking 100 degrees, but the topless mountains we saw all through New Mexico and Arizona multiplied and grew even larger. I never thought a rock could be so beautiful, with the painted-on colored layers, growing in the shades of reds and coral. The mountains were all washed by the red sand that is plentiful in Utah. The sand is as slippery under foot as white beach sand, and the wind does blow it onto the road, just as it would by the ocean. But this sand is red and created from the wind blasting against the red rocks that create the mountains.

We stopped at the visitor's center and met a very knowledgeable man who also rides, and he suggested going north through Zion National Park, as opposed to the southern route the Garmin was suggesting. He also explained the difference between a national park and a national monument. A park has roads built through it so many people can drive through and enjoy the park. A National Monument is left as Mother Nature has painted it. No manmade anything to change the land. There is so much land that is still owned by the federal government out west. The vastness and beauty of this untouched land is just mind blowing.

We stopped in Kanab, Utah, at a lovely family-owned restaurant called Houston's. If you are ever in Kanab, you have to try their homemade raspberry pie a la mode. It was the best pie I or Bonz (who is a raspberry nut) has ever eaten. We also stopped at a cute boutique next door, which had many things I would have bought if I'd had the room.

After lunch, we headed north to cut through Zion National Park on our way to Hurricane. I was not really expecting much I had not already seen, but again, I was wrong. There are the most beautiful red mountains of topless red rocks, sliced like shale and sandblasted into some of the most beautiful shapes, while still towering over the red road we were riding on. We saw buffalo, wild mountain goats climbing the rock, and long horned sheep as we rode along. To get into Zion we rode through a tunnel carved into the mountain.

I thought this was really cool until we went to leave and rode through a very long and twisted tunnel carved through a very large mountain with a few large windows carved into the tunnel. In between the two tunnels were some of the most beautiful and breathtaking views I have ever seen. I really would have to say that Zion National Park is an amusement park made with bikers in mind created by Mother Nature herself, with all the twisting and curving roads and changing scenery at every new angle. It was such a perfect day; I was a little disappointed when we actually reached our destination and stopped riding for the day.

That was short lived, as we were meeting our friends from our HOG group, Gary and Sue, for dinner. They are on vacation in Utah and our plan was to meet up tomorrow and stay with them. They came back to Hurricane earlier today than originally expected, and it was great to start to catch up on everyone's adventures on the road. Today was an awesome day, and I have a feeling tomorrow will be even better.

Assessing changes in our second quarter on the road:
Observations and speculations: (days 25-41)

So far this quarter we have been through Texas, New Mexico, Arizona, and have just made it to Utah. This part of the country is not only beautiful, but very hot. Of course, this part of the country is going through a heat wave this year so bad that in June more than 50 airline flights were grounded in Phoenix, Arizona. I learned that hot air is less dense and this affects the output of engines, causing them to need longer runways. It also reduces an airplane's ability to climb at a necessary rate to avoid things like mountains and towers. We've kept an eye on the engine temps during this time and luckily have had no issues with the bikes overheating.

The ever-changing scenery in this part of the country is so mind-blowingly beautiful and vast. I enjoyed seeing the working pump jacks, windmills, and land being farmed, all at the same time on the same land in Texas. It was nice to see how they incorporated so many different aspects of energy together to make them work. The beauty of the topless mountains and the desert are breathtaking. Route 66 was a lot of fun to check out. We took the original Route 66 as often as possible, and stopped at all the roadside attractions we could find. When we finally had to leave Route 66 to head north, it was a little sad knowing our little treasure hunt was over. But the beauty of riding along the Grand Canyon and the exquisite beauty of Zion brought us a new zest for adventure.

Bonz and I have settled into a nice routine, and are both more comfortable with changing plans at a dime's notice. We have both gotten better at stopping to see something that may interest us. Our focus is less aimed at where we want to end up and more focused on what fun and interesting things we can find along the way. This is very good for us as a couple. At home we seem to be so focused on what we need to do that we forget to stop and play and enjoy the here and now. We also get so wrapped up in what we are trying to accomplish that we don't always hear what the other person is trying to say.

In a long-term relationship, I believe it sometimes takes a conscious effort to make fun a priority, and we have been very successful at re-learning how to do this through the southwest. Learning to listen to each other and checking each other's heartbeat has helped to bring back the close trust that we seem to have taken for granted through time. Every day is not perfect, but we make the best of what we have and move forward from there. Some days the heat just gets to you, and when either of us can hear the other getting a little snippy, instead of taking it personally, we suggest it may be time to stop.

On breaks in shady spots, we are able to talk and find out what the issue is and decide as a couple what we want to do to make the other as comfortable as possible. Sometimes it is just time for Bonz to eat, and one time it was finding some shade before I passed out, being that I was suffering from a small bout of dehydration. Bonz seems to be able to handle the heat much better than I do. Spending so much time together having fun has allowed us to relax and feel more comfortable with each other, and brought back that close friendship we had when we were first dating.

An idea of our spending for this quarter: so far we have spent approximately $1700 on lodging, $900 on food, and about $330 on gas. Of course, we have spent $1300 more on incidentals. So our total for this quarter is about $4230. (Not including new tires).

Day Forty-Two – Hurricane, Utah
(7/11/17)

Well, today was fun, with an unexpected twist. We packed up from the motel and headed over to Gary and Sue's; we will be staying with them in their very beautiful Toy Hauler for a few weeks. After a wonderful homemade breakfast that Sue cooked, we started out on a run to the mountains. Every time my bike went over 70 (the speed limit in Utah is 80), the front end would start to wobble. It did this the last time I put new tires on it, but Harvey's Harley Davidson dealer in Macedon, NY, got rid of the wobble when they changed the warped rotors. It was making me nervous, so we turned around and headed back to Zion Harley Davidson. They were great there and took it right in to look at it.

While we were waiting, we decided it was a great time to shop. We found some cooling vests, and picked up a few. They are very popular in the desert. You soak them in water for five minutes and put them on and they keep you cool until all the water dries up (about 5 hours). I had read about them, but had never actually seen one before. In NY, we are usually trying to find things to keep us warm.

While we were waiting, we met our first girl traveling long distance alone. She was riding from California to Florida. We have run into many men traveling alone doing a long-distance run, but it was so nice to see a woman doing the same. It would take a lot of balls to do that (man or woman). I am very blessed that my husband loves to ride as much as I do. While we were exchanging road stories, another couple riding long distance rode up and joined us. (Distance is always obvious by the bags tied to the back of the bikes). They were riding from Florida in a circle to California and across the top of the country, back down and around to get back home, and were sleeping in hammocks. You can find his videos of his run on YouTube under Hammocks and Harleys. He was set up with three GoPros on his bike, getting all the good angles of his run. He edits them so all you watch is the really good stuff. I could watch videos like that all day, but I am sure most people would get bored if they were not edited down to a smaller time frame like he does.

The guys at Zion Harley Davidson tightened up the front forks and changed the fork oil. The front end feels a lot tighter, but my ghost wobble is still there. They assured me that everything is good and the front end is safe (the tire will not fall off), so I'm just going to live with it. It only shows up over 70, so I think I may ask Santa for a wider front tire for Christmas. But the bike no longer has its clunk when I hit the brakes, so all is good.

It was too late for the original ride we'd set out for today, so we came back to camp and had dinner and got some much-needed laundry done. Tomorrow we will get up and do it again. Amen.

Day Forty-Three – Hurricane, Utah
(7/12/17)

I could never live in Utah. In order to get anything done before the heat kicks in, you have to get up so early! We were up at 7:00 a.m. to beat the heat, and were totally successful! We headed out to

Cedar Breaks, which is a national monument in Utah. This is the first stage of making it a national park. The land is owned by the federal government, and in 1933 President Roosevelt established this national monument to preserve it as it is for future generations. There is a three-mile wide amphitheater that can be seen from the park entrance which is just spectacular. The ride through Cedar Breaks did actually get cold, as it is 10,000 feet high at one point. Great way to beat the heat! The pines were badly scorched in some places and charred in others. The parks department is in the process of putting out the forest fires in the area. The road helped contain the fire in most places, but in some the fire made it across. It is so very sad, as the park is so beautifully covered in pine trees.

For lunch, we stopped at the cutest diner (I love diners), the Galaxy of Hatch. Their sign says, "Bikers, Burgers, and Beds!" The owner came out and we were talking to him and he showed us the motel rooms. They were exquisite, from the Harley mural on the wall, with the Harley bedding and ceiling fan, to the use of tool boxes for a dresser. The rooms are absolutely adorable! And breakfast at the diner is included in the room cost. After eating motel breakfasts for over a month, I found this a glorious perk, especially since the food at the diner is very good.

I absolutely love places with personality. Especially in this world of corporate cleansing to try and please everyone, all personality seems to have been washed away. So it is such a treat to see someone do something that they love and not fear adding a part of their own personality to it. It was a very refreshing change. We totally enjoyed our visit there, and would definitely call the Galaxy at Hatch a definite do-over (Meaning definitely worth a repeat visit).

We headed down the road to go to Bryce Canyon, as it is not far from Hatch, but the lightning and black cloud pouring rain down on the mountain made us change our mind, so off we went to Zion, as Gary was telling us they have a bus that goes to the bottom of the Canyon, which we had not seen yet. And another beautiful ride through the bikers' paradise that is Zion Nation Park will never be turned down by me.

First we rode through the most beautiful rock formations, including two tunnels carved into the mountains that we rode through the other day, and then headed over to the bus tour of the bottom part. As cars cannot go down this part, a bus is your only option. It was pretty cool to listen to the hikers describe their adventures of the day, much like bikers do when they get together, discussing which part of their journey they would recommend for fellow hikers and what they would not suggest. I guess we are not really that different, especially when it comes to befriending others with your shared passions.

Today was another awesome day, so hopefully tomorrow we will get up and do it again. Amen.

Day Forty-Four – Las Vegas, Nevada
(7/13/17)

Las Vegas, Baby! The weatherman said it was only going to be 105 degrees today, and I had a man to marry, so we all climbed into Gary's truck and enjoyed being driven in the air conditioning. Having never been to Las Vegas before, we wanted to be able to function when we got there. Our first stop was Graceland Wedding Chapel. Because what is a trip to Vegas without an Elvis Wedding?

Bonz and I are already married, so this time it was all for fun. We got the basic package, DVD, Pictures, and Elvis. By the time we were done, our $200 package cost close to $500 bucks, but we had fun. They really have this same-day wedding thing down in Vegas. Our Elvis was a very good Elvis. We have seen some impersonators that were not very close, but he was a good Elvis, with a great voice.

After the wedding, we headed to the local Harley dealer and had fun shopping there. The dealership was huge, and had lots to choose from. We decided to grab a cab from there down to the Harley Restaurant to grab a bite to eat, but it no longer existed. Our cab driver was from Russia, and we had a nice conversation on our way there. He explained that it took him two years to get all his paperwork approved to get him, his wife, and daughter here. He absolutely loves Las Vegas. It would take a lot of balls to pick up and move to another country where they don't even speak your language. It makes you wonder what it was like in Russia to want to do that. Having never been there, I can only guess.

I have nothing against immigrants, being that most Americans were immigrants at one time. I have nothing but respect for people that follow their dreams, and sadness that people are having such hard times learning to compromise and accept people that are different than them. I personally love the differences I see in people; it allows me to pick up the things I love and leave the parts I don't, making life a little more interesting with each new friend I have met. It just makes me realize just how very blessed I am to be born in a country that I love.

The Rainforest Café was nearby, so all was good! Had a wonderful meal and headed out to the casinos to make our donations. After trying our luck at a few casinos, the sun was starting to go down so we headed off to Fremont Street to people watch. And let me tell you, there are a lot of things to see on Fremont Street if you like to watch the weird. So many people dressed (or completely undressed), that are happy for you to take a picture with them for a price. There is a lot of poverty seen in Los Vegas; the contrast is very obvious against the glitter and glamor of the casinos.

The one thing about Vegas is everything is for sale for a price. They also had a few bandstands with some pretty awesome musicians playing. They also had a zipline you could ride right down the strip. There is always something to see on Fremont Street. Could spend lots of time enjoying the view there, but it was getting late so we headed back to Utah, as it was a two-hour ride back to our temporary home.

Day Forty-Five – Hurricane, Utah
(7/14/17)

After all the crazy that was Vegas, today was a nice relaxing day. I slept half the day away, not getting up till 10:30 a.m. felt great! I have not slept that late in ages. I took my time enjoying a cup of coffee and Bonz cooked breakfast for everyone while I wrote my blog for yesterday, as I went directly to bed and did not pass Go when we got home last night.

We went to Wally world (Walmart) to get Bonz a bathing suit that stays on (kind of important), and a few other things we needed. Then we relaxed with Gary and Sue, enjoying their company before we all headed out to dinner. Dinner was excellent; we went to The Gun Barrel for steaks. They also served buffalo and elk, but I stuck with Beef, as I know I like that. The restaurant was very adorable with the dead animal skins and heads on the walls, and huge exposed beams. I love that mountain décor; for some reason, it is very comforting.

After dinner, we went to a Johnny Depp movie, *Pirates of the Caribbean: Dead Men Tell No Tales.* It was really good. It is still very hot in Utah, so a night at the movies was a nice reprieve from the heat after a lovely dinner. So now I am heading to bed so we can get up and do it again. Amen.

Day Forty-Six – Hurricane, Utah
(7/15/17)

Today we checked out the North Rim of the Grand Canyon. The North Rim is open to the public from May 15th to October 15th and is only visited by 10 % of the people that visit the Grand Canyon each year. It is about 130 miles from where we are staying each way. We all packed up in Gary's truck as the weather in Hurricane was already close to 100 when we left. On our way here we missed going into the North Rim because of the heat, and I really wanted to see it, as we are so close, and I don't know if I'll ever get the chance again. I never understood too hot to ride until I came to the desert in the summer time.

It is spectacular, and huge, and pictures just don't do it any justice. We ate at the Grand Canyon Lodge, and the food was excellent. We had the soup/salad/sandwich buffet. After lunch, we hiked the Bright Angel Point Trail. The trail was not very long going down, but the walk back up was a lot more difficult. It could have something to do with my smoking, but we are not going there, so we will blame it on the lack of oxygen at 8000 feet. At one point, you are looking down the Canyon on both sides, which can make a person like me a little leery. Of course, it did not bother Sue as she sat with her feet hanging over the edge. A place like that can really make you feel small, and the colors of the Canyon are spectacular. Do you know there are electric lines running down the Canyon? I definitely would not want that job.

There are also the cutest log cabins at the North Rim that you can rent for $200 a night, and a campground that had lots of trees for shade. We did not get a tour of the cabins this time, but I looked them up online and they look very nice.

When we got home we ordered pizza and started to pack up, as we are moving to Colorado tomorrow. The lower heat will be better, but the weather app says thunderstorms all next week. But as we have learned, the showers never last long in the mountains, so all is good.

Day Forty-Seven – Tuba City, Arizona
(7/16/17)

We woke up early today and packed up. I got to see how Gary loads the bikes in the back of the camper. Our bedroom easily turned into a garage, and the bikes load right up the ramp and into a wheel lock. It was pretty cool. After many years of loading and unloading the Flathead into pickup trucks, the setup of the camper is really pretty sweet. Gary usually does it himself, but the bikes had to load at an angle, and we were there, so we helped. What a beautiful camper they have, and we have had so much fun exploring Utah with them, and will be meeting them in Colorado.

We headed out through the piney forest back to Arizona and through the desert. We stopped for water at a gas station in the desert, and ran into a bunch of bikers. We had a nice talk. One said,

"Well, you must have researched that it is monsoon season in the Colorado Mountains now." Well, my timing on this trip has most likely not been the best, but we have enjoyed every minute of it so far. When you only have one window, you take it. Even if it means riding through the south during hurricane season, the desert in July, and the monsoon season in the Rocky's. Bonz always eats well during rainy season, so all is good.

We hit the half waypoint to Colorado and decided to grab something to eat, get a room, and cool down a bit. I'm a little excited to get out of the desert. Have I told you it is hot here? I mean, really hot?! Well, I'm signing off so we can get an early start and try to beat the heat tomorrow.

Day Forty-Eight – Mesa Verde, Colorado
(7/17/17)

Today was our last day driving through the desert. We got up early to try to beat the heat and were on the road by a little after 8:00. The morning weather was nice, as it is pretty cool in the desert in the morning. I soaked the cooling vest in the sink and let it drip dry in the tub for about ten minutes before I put it on. This way my pants were less soaked when I put it on, and I did not leave a watery mess in the room. I may never need to wear it again, but it was worth every penny for the few days I wore it.

The desert is so very alive and beautiful, and so very not what I pictured it to be before I actually saw it. I think I expected a lot more white sand and a lot less vegetation. It is some of the most beautiful scenery, stretching out forever. I never realized how much land in this country is uninhabited. The BML (Bureau of Land Management) handles 12.2 million archers of public land in Arizona alone (not including the 17.5 million of subsurface acres). Then there is the Fort Mojave Indian Reservation, which is another 23,669 acres in Arizona. You can see forever and never see a house. But you know a gas station is coming up when the speed limit on the road reduces from 65 to 45 mph.

We rode past the Four Corners, where the four states come together, and turned a corner and the mountains changed. They are no longer the topless (mesa's) mountains of the desert. They are now the foothills of the Rocky Mountains. The change came pretty quickly after passing the Colorado line. So did the cooler air, which was very appreciated by Bonz and I as we climbed in elevation.

We arrived at Gary and Sue's new campsite in Colorado and had a wonderful meal that Sue cooked, lasagna. It was fabulous, and we enjoyed playing a few hands of cards. Today was a good day. I will miss the beauty of the desert, but to be honest, I don't think I will miss the heat (at least until December in NY). Tomorrow we have lots of new sights to discover, so I am signing off for today.

Day Forty-Nine – Mesa, Verde, Colorado
(7/18/2017)

Today was an awesome day. We got up early and headed out to ride a 250-mile loop through the mountains that included the Million Dollar Highway. It is another favorite road for bikers, and quite well- known. For my non-biker friends that are reading this, I have copied some information below.

"In the state of Colorado of the United States of America, there's a special highway built in the late 1880s: the Million Dollar Highway, part of the San Juan Skyway. It's one of the nation's most spectacular drives. You'll be on the "outside" for a while with a hell of a view to your right (let the passenger look. You'll want to watch the road). Forget standard driving safety measures like guardrails and shoulders; there aren't any on this stretch, so swerving off the road is not advised!

From Durango, through Silverton and Ouray, to Ridgway, the highway delivers jaw-dropping vista after vista. It was cut from the side of the mountain and became known as the "Million Dollar Highway." It's one of the most scenic drives in the USA. The Million Dollar Highway stretches for about 25 miles (40 km) in western Colorado and follows the route of U.S. 550 between Silverton and Ouray, Colorado. It is part of the San Juan Skyway. Between Durango and Silverton, the Skyway loosely parallels the Durango and Silverton Narrow Gauge Railroad. The road climbs up to three very high mountain passes. Coal Bank Pass (10,640 ft. /3,240 m); Molas Pass (10,970 ft. /3,340 m); and Red Mountain Pass (11,018 ft. /3,358 m). The road is fine as long as you don't drive too fast for conditions. But if you do, the consequences are severe." (http://www.dangerousroads.org/north-america/usa/635-million-dollar-highway-usa.html)

Why is it that when someone says, "Honey, whatever you do, don't look down," the first thing I do is immediately look down? Yep, that's me. The views of the mountains for the ride were absolutely spectacular and fun, but listen to Bonz and don't look down. The cliff started where the white line of the highway ended. We were sandwiched between hugging the mountain on one side and a huge cliff on the other, as the road twisted through the mountain. It would have made an awesome picture, but there is absolutely no place to stop. The Rocky Mountains show hints of the topless mountains (mesa's) of Arizona, but look like they added hats (peaks) and clothes (dirt and trees) to them, but every once in a while, you can see the layered rocks peeking through the trees, or hugging the road.

At one point, there was a stretch of road that was freshly oiled and stoned. This, with the lack of guardrails, made for a little scary streak of the ride. Anyone that has ever ridden a motorcycle in freshly laid stone knows that the tires of the machine just do not like those conditions. Then you add the switchbacks, curves, and drop offs, and it gets a little hairy. But hopefully they will be done with the roadwork by the time you take this ride.

It truly fascinates me how the landscape can change as we ride through this wonderful country. Just 100 miles away is the desert with a temperature over 100 degrees, and today we left with our coats, gloves and chaps on. The temperature drops as the elevation gets higher. We visited the highest Harley Davidson store in the world today in Silverton, Colorado. It is definitely a cute little ski town, tucked neatly in a tiny valley surrounded by mountains. Silverton was once a mining town for gold, but also silver; now it is famous for skiing. Shaun White trained there for the 2010 Olympics. In 2000 the population was 531 according to the census. It is quite cute and has a train from Durango to Silverton, which originated for mining, but is now used for tourism. We also had a very good Mexican lunch while we were there.

After lunch, the sky quickly changed to dark and rain was imminent, so we decided we were going to head out on our way. We were lucky for most of the ride, but the rain caught up to us not far from Telluride. By the time we made it to town, we were completely soaked. The temperature had dropped, and we pulled into a gas station there to wait out the worst of the storm. Do you know that the thunder is louder at the top of the mountain? This is not a proven scientific fact that I know of, just personal opinion. We also saw a huge group of elk grazing in the field behind the gas station we were camped out at. I found the name of the town amusing and highly suggest opening a diner called I Can. (Get it? I-can-tell-u-ride?) Okay, what can I say? I was amusing myself.

When the thunderstorm calmed down to a whisper, we decided to head back to camp; we only had about 80 miles left and one more mountain to pass. As we rode past the snow-capped mountains surrounding us, soaked to the bone, it made me think of home. Where else (other than Buffalo) can you find snow this time of year? Not often, but it happens.

As we descended the mountain peak, the temperature slowly got warmer, and we were mostly dry by the time we got back to camp, except our jeans; they never fully dry. We decided to head out to Wally World (Walmart) and grab a bite to eat, after changing into dry clothes. The ride was awesome; dinner was good; and the memories are priceless. Gary, as always was the perfect road captain.

Day Fifty – Mesa Verde, Colorado
(7/19/17)

Today we are taking a nice down day and spending it at the campsite. Bonz and Sue are napping and Gary is working on his laptop, so I thought I would start my blog early today. This trip has actually been a lot more fun and eye opening than I had expected. I am not a planned person. When things overwhelm me, I find I have to break them down into little pieces, so we just looked at a map and got a general idea of where we would like to go, and winged it as we traveled. We left lots of extra time so if we loved something or somewhere, we could stay an extra day or two. We have not made all the stops we originally planned to hit because of rain or heat. But we have learned to listen to each other, and not push too hard, and this works for us. Remember, everyone is different, and our goal was just to see the US and have an enjoyable trip. So far, we have exceeded in our goal.

As we meet people along the way, they are all so happy to make suggestions. We have tried to hit most of the places suggested to us and have not been disappointed. This has many times altered our trip for the better. Remember that the locals always know best. Best places to eat, stay overnight, and best things to see in the area. We have met many wonderful people everywhere we have stopped, some friendlier than others, but most have been respectful. We have been placed in our own room at some restaurants because they fear bikers, but I have no problem with the added privacy. It is all in the attitude. Their bad attitude does not have to ruin my good day. I even had a child in his twenties scream out "Fuck you" to me as I sat in a gas station on my bike waiting for Bonz to come back with a couple of waters. Of course, I returned with, "Sorry, not your type, I'm not inflatable" which brought a few laughs from others filling their cars at the same station. One man even came over and apologized for the kid, and he did not know him either.

When people hate me because they see me sitting on my motorcycle, it is their loss. Their predisposed impressions of who I am are their issues, not mine. The newspapers have been having a hay day over the past twenty years trying to tell the public how horrible bikers are with their propaganda, and it really is mostly fiction. They need a villain, and assume they can destroy any group with their propaganda. The truth is the areas that accept bikers find that bikers are adults and know how to police themselves. We show up on vacations with pockets full of money and love to spend it in places that accept us. At rallies, the people that are most out of control do not even ride motorcycles, but show up to cause trouble because this is their misconception of what a biker is.

We are bad ass because we can handle what is thrown at us, like fresh stone on oiled roads, and thunderstorms that show up suddenly, with no safe place to stop. We push ourselves by riding the most dangerous roads, and actually ride long distances to be able to do this. We have to tackle teenagers texting or moms in mini vans screaming at their kids and not paying attention to where they are aiming their cages of death, and there are still a few that think it is fun to try and run a motorcycle off the road. The truth is, we are just people that you actually run into every day, and because we are not wearing our protective gear at the time you have no idea. So many people stop and talk to us about bikes they used to own, or bikes they still ride. It is a tight-knit community that has more members than you could ever dream. There are definitely many styles of riders, and I love to talk to all other riders, as they all have a story if you are willing to listen, and sometimes they share their experience, strengths, and hopes. And other times you can find really great roads; because this life is all about the journey, not the destination.

So next time you assume someone is a bad person because they are different than you, or they have tattoos or piercings, or you have heard rumors that that type of person is really bad, try talking to them. Everyone has a story, and when you learn to listen, I mean really listen, you may find they have something very interesting to say, and you may learn something new that you can add to your journey to make it even more wonderful. We are all a little different, and yet all a lot the same. Stop trying to control others and take responsibility for your own actions and you may find your own freedom in doing so.

Day Fifty-One – Mesa Verde, Colorado
(7/20/2017)

I woke up last night to the most awesome lightshow ever put on by God. It reminded me of a disco strobe light, one lightning strike after another covering the tops of the mountains surrounding us. I have a massive love for thunder and lightning storms; I find them very comforting. It reminds me that God rides a Harley, and when the angels kick the bikes to life you can hear the thunder roll and watch the fire from their pipes come shooting down to earth as they enjoy their ride. Mother Nature can be so splendid sometimes, but I must admit I like the storms best when my bike is parked.

Today the boys took a run to the Harley Davidson dealer down by the Four Corners where four states come together. So now Bonz has an excuse for his mileage to be over one hundred miles more than me (although I am not fully giving up on the thought of him sleep riding). Sue enjoyed a nice quiet day at camp all by herself, and I rode into Dolores to see an old friend from high school that I have not seen in close to forty years.

The weather was great when I left, so I had short sleeves and a pair of jeans on. Of course, I got lost and the ride there took me over an hour. The GPS put me one place (no idea where in the middle of nowhere) and my phone tried to send me to another spot about twenty miles from where the GPS sent me. The internet ended up with zero bars, so I turned back to the town and did it the old-fashioned way: I asked directions. Of course, they were correct, and nowhere near where the GPS or the Google maps on my phone sent me.

I finally arrived an hour late, but I made it! It was so nice to see Jan after all these years, and see she was still the same wonderful person I remembered. This world has not taken her wonderful zest for life that I have always loved about her. We decided to head down off the mountain and go to town for a bite to eat. She has never ridden on a Harley before, and I absolutely love to have the pleasure of sharing my passion with someone that has never tried it before. We felt a few teardrops on our way down the mountain, but town was only a few miles away. We had a lovely lunch and enjoyed telling stories from the last forty years of our lives, as the sky outside the window decided to unload quite a bit of water onto the ground (notice how I refuse to admit it is raining? One of the angels must have left the gas pump running on full blast for a while.)

It finally calmed down outside and I rode Jan back up the mountain to re-join her friends. On the mountain top where she was staying, they had had a massive hailstorm while we only saw the rain just a few miles away. The remnants of that storm were scattered on the ground like snow when we arrived. I decided I better head back while the window of calm was still in the air. The sky was still pretty black, but the lightning show to my right on the way home was again spectacular, especially since I only had a few teardrops coming from the sky, but the road spray from the puddles left from the downpour successfully drenched me.

If you love to watch a good storm, Mesa Verde, Colorado, is the place to be this time of year. There can be close to one hundred lightning strikes within a minute. I tried to do a Facebook live on Bonz's phone yesterday, but when the lightning would strike it would kill the connection, so it came out very choppy with no lightning. Try it sometime; it was pretty weird. Like not filming a vampire, you cannot Facebook live a lightning strike. God just edited them all out.

I got the bike parked for the night about ten minutes before the rain decided to grace us with her presence, and the angels went for another ride. Sue cooked another awesome meal, and we watched the Wild Hogs movie, as it was so fitting. I absolutely love that movie; maybe next trip we can go all the way to California.

Day Fifty-Two – Gunnison, Colorado
(7/21/2017)

We packed up and headed out this morning. As staying with Gary and Sue was the longest we have been in one place (even if it was two locations) over the past month and a half, it felt like we were leaving home. As we looked in the rearview mirror and saw Gary and Sue, I felt like I was saying goodbye to family. We thoroughly enjoyed their company over the past week. Gary has this magical knack for knowing the best roads, and has never gotten us lost. He is definitely one of the best road captains I have ridden with. To me, being a person that gets lost in her own backyard, I find this fascinating. I am always so impressed when someone has a gift I was not born with. It will be fun to get together and share war stories when we return home.

Well, the weatherman said there was a fifty percent chance of rain, and someone said if the weatherman says fifty percent chance when you're in the mountains you will only get wet fifty percent of the ride. Well, we only got wet about ten percent of our ride, so today was a good day.

The ride through the mountains was beautiful. We did need to stop to put the rain gear on as the black clouds were surrounding us, threatening a very bad storm. The rain came, with the chill mostly at the top of the mountain, but as we descended the weather got warmer and we quickly dried off. Route 50 was absolutely wonderful with slow winding curves meandering around the mountains, through more untouched BLM land. We passed some beautiful lakes tucked beautifully into the mountain, and the lack of cottages surrounding it looked so foreign to us. But the natural state of the lake was so impressive. There was some road construction in a few spots that left lines of cars stopped as the construction brought the traffic down to one lane, but the rough road was not too bad on the motorcycles. Being that we had no time table to keep, this was a nice way to stop and enjoy the scenery.

We made it to Gunnison just in time to feed my Bonz. This was perfect timing, as we went to High Alpine Brewing Company, where Cassie is a manager. We had not seen her since she and my daughter Lindsey graduated high school. Cassie moved out west after high school, and I love her free spirit. We enjoyed a nice dinner with her and will reconnect tomorrow for lunch.

We settled into the motel and after a nice long hot shower, I am going to enjoy a good night's sleep in our new temporary home. I do find that sleep usually comes easy while on our journey. This way we can get up and do it again. Amen.

Day Fifty-Three - Gunnison, Colorado
(7/22/2017)

We picked up Cassie this morning and took a ride to Crested Butte. We only hit a few teardrops on our way up the mountain, but the air definitely had a chill to it. Crested Butte is a cute little ski town that is popular in the summer for hiking, and known for the wildflowers that grow on the mountain. It started as a mining town and used to produce 1000 tons of coal a day, before it closed down the mine in 1952. Cassie is a wealth of information about the mountain, and she truly loves this area. Her favorite season is snow, and being this high in the mountains, she gets a lot of that.

We walked around and checked out the town for a while before stopping for lunch at a cute little restaurant. The food was good, but seemed to take forever, which was okay as this gave us time to talk and also allowed the rain to stop. After lunch, we headed to the ski resort to check it out. The ski lift was taking people up the mountain to see the view and bring hikers and mountain bikers up the mountain. I was quite surprised by the amount of people milling around. Being that I am not a skier, I have decided that I like ski resorts in the summer time. It is very beautiful there.

We enjoyed a rain-free ride through the mountains to bring Cassie home to get ready for work. It was so nice seeing her again, and seeing how well she is doing. One thing about these high elevations is that you get tired easily. So we decided to head back to the motel and take a nap; next thing I knew it was the middle of the night …That day went fast!

Day Fifty-Four – Aurora, Colorado
(7/23/2017)

Today was a perfect day. We stayed at the Western Motel in Gunnison for the past two days, and totally enjoyed our stay. The couple that owned the motel were very sweet, and the motel is obviously very well loved. Our room was not only very clean; it was also very spacious, and adorably decorated. And the coffee was excellent, and good coffee is so very important in the morning. We packed up and headed out over the mountain and through the pass to Aurora, next door to Denver.

The ride was absolutely spectacular. Remember that when you ride a motorcycle, the ride is absolutely the highlight of the trip when you find a good road, and today the roads were awesome. The view from the top of the mountain was just breathtaking. It was a little chilly at the top of the mountain, but quickly warmed as we descended, down the long curvy beautiful road. The Rocky Mountains are absolutely beautiful. There were a few more cars on my road (I guess I got used to having the road to myself), than I would have preferred. But it was Sunday and people were all heading back home to the Front Range (Boulder, Denver area at the base of the mountains). We hit absolutely no rain on this trip through the mountains today, which just made the trip that much more enjoyable.

We stopped at a small restaurant next to a gas station, Tony's, along the way. It was run by a man and his son, and we had the best burgers we have had in quite a while. I love small family-owned restaurants; they are always my favorites.

When we got to Aurora, we called James and he met us at Chili's for a nice meal, and great company. I was very glad he did not have plans tonight as I gave him about two hours' notice that we would be in town (I have never been very good at planning ahead). It has been a while since we have seen him, so it was nice catching up. So far it seems that we have more friends in this state than any others. After being away from home for almost two months, it is nice to visit with friends when we can. Today was just a perfect day.

Day Fifty-Five – Fort Lupton, Colorado
(7/24/2017)

Today was a fun play day. We started out at the Mile High Harley Davidson dealer in Aurora, Colorado. I am collecting pins from our trip. I have plans for a new lampshade for the living room when I get home. Hey, when you have no room left on the bike, but you still love to shop at Harley dealers, you make concessions. Where there is a will, there is always a way.

We headed out to Boulder, Colorado next. I used to live there for a little while in 1980. It is now a city. It looks so very different. We had lunch at Pasta Jay's on Pearl Street, which made Bonz very happy. He loves pasta. We went to the Pearl Street mall and watched the street performers, as one of my favorite pastimes is people watching. There were a few guitar players, our first skateboarder we have seen in Colorado, and a hacky sack champion that was having fun lighting chairs on fire and placing them on his face. At least the important parts of Boulder have survived.

They have added a few more blocks to the mall, a small water fountain for the kids to play in, and some large rocks for the small ones to climb. There were also many benches for people to people watch, so I was not the only one enjoying this pastime. I don't think the mall used to be as family friendly as it is now. I also don't think it had as many people visiting as it does now either. But it is still a must to visit if you are ever in Boulder.

I found a motel about twenty miles from Boulder, in Fort Lupton, and I had never been there so that was where we headed off to next. We ended up in rush hour traffic on what we thought were backroads. I guess we were headed in the same direction as most of the people that work in the Boulder area. Traffic moves pretty nicely until they stick a traffic light in the middle of nowhere, and then traffic seems to back up for miles until you get through the light. Then traffic moves fine again until the next light. The same thing seemed to happen when we were heading out of the mountains on Sunday. I have never seen a traffic light create such havoc before.

When we pulled into the motel, there was a group of people sitting in chairs on the small lawn that the motel had. It reminded me of the smoking area at high school, and because I met so many cool people at the smoking area at high school, we just had to join in on the party. We met a retired sheriff on vacation with his daughter; a fiber installer who was traveling for work; a mechanic who also fought in the UFC (Ultimate Fighting Competition); and a few others whose stories I did not get. There was no beer or drugs being consumed there, just a lot of travelers enjoying each other's company. Bonz and I enjoyed their pictures and stories about their beautiful bikes and hot rods that they have left at home, and exchanging our stories. I don't think we have enjoyed a motel this much since we were in the Smoky Mountains. I love meeting new people as we travel and learning their stories, when they are willing to share, is always such a gift.

Day Fifty-Six – Fort Lupton, Colorado
(7/25/2017)

Well, the room was clean and cheap and that evil necessity, laundry, was calling our name, so we decided to book the room for another day. This motel does not have a guest laundry, but there is a laundromat just a few blocks down. We filled a bag and headed off for some sudsy excitement. Well, it really was not very exciting, but clean clothes are always a good thing.

When we were done, we came back to the room and got some reading done. It was a nice lazy day. Around six, we got together with our new friends and decided to have a grill out in the parking lot. One of the guys had a grill at his shop and brought it over and Bonz and I headed to the store to pick up some burgers, sausage, and hots. We also grabbed some chips and potato salad. My kind of party: catered. It was fun, and we met more people. The weather decided it wanted a nice light cry during our parking lot party, but this did not even put a dent in our fun.

There are about 7000 people that live in this town, but there really are not a lot of things going on downtown. Traffic getting here had such long lines, but not many people hang out in town, so there is not much traffic here. I am under the impression that most people here work in the Denver/Boulder area. So it is definitely a commuter town. All in all, today was a good day.

Day Fifty-Seven – Loveland, Colorado
(7/26/2017)

We woke up and packed. The plan was to visit the Harley dealers moving north in Colorado. When I had everything tied up on the bike, I realized I could not find my goggles. They are not just goggles; they are prescription goggles. I am a little blind without them. I thought about this for a few minutes and figured we were headed to the Harley Dealer, and I have at least seen bifocal goggles there before. Then I would only be half blind, so off we went.

Stopped at High Country Harley Davidson and found a pair of riding glasses with bifocals, but they were sunglasses. I never wear sunglasses, as I find them hard to see through. But seeing the GPS is kind of important, as we have no idea where we are going without it. The people were very nice, but I was getting a little depressed. I tried Googling same-day eye ware, and called. Turns out same-day eye ware has to send out for lenses for goggles, so it would take one to two weeks for them to come in.

We had no intention of hanging out that long here, so we headed to Walmart to see if I could order the goggles and have them sent to South Dakota, and I would pick them up there. Turns out that the company cannot do that. If you order eye ware at one store, the glasses have to go to that store and cannot be sent to another Walmart for pick up.

Argggg. What is a blind person to do without glasses if they are out of town and have lost theirs? I even tried calling my eye doctor back home, but he would have to order them and it could take longer than we have in South Dakota to get them. And the prescription is old, and they cost about $400.00. This is turning out to be a real problem.

We headed to the next Harley Dealer, Thunder Mountain, which was actually pretty awesome. They have an amphitheater at the dealership, and have concerts and rallies there. The people were so friendly, and I was just so grumpy. I hate being blind, and the thought of riding 4000 miles without really being able to see was just a little nerve racking for me. Maybe food would help.

We found a little deli and had a couple of subs that were awesome, and a little larger than I should have finished. But when they taste that good, I finish it. I came up with the idea of heading to a lumber store and picking up a clear set of safety glasses, with bifocals. At least then I could clearly see the GPS and it would be easier to see the blur in front of me going down the road.

We found a Lowes and picked up a pair, walked outside, and it started raining. That was it. I quit for today. This was turning out to be a terrible, horrible, very bad, no good day that I should have stayed in bed for. So we decided to get a room. Checking my phone was not helping my day, as it was having major issues. It was jumping and opening pages I did not want to see. The heat over the past month has taken its toll on my phone, and it definitely needs to be replaced, but not today.

I found a room with a pool, as I thought this might help me out of my bad mood. Bonz was an angel, as he kept his cool and did not let me swirl into an even worse mood. If one of us is having a bad day, we can get through it. If both of us are in bad moods, this is very bad. We checked into the hotel and found that they also had a hot tub, and it looked pretty inviting. We unpacked and when I pulled my laptop out of the bag, my goggles were wrapped up in the plastic I use to protect the electronics from the rain. After spending all day trying to figure out how to replace them, unsuccessfully, this was a good find.

Bonz took a nap and I headed down to the indoor pool area. I walked outside to have a smoke, and lo and behold, there was the most beautiful rainbow right outside the door. It made me realize just how lucky I was, and reminded me that very rarely does a worst-case scenario ever come true. So all that stress I put myself under was totally unnecessary. I do believe that this was not the first day I have ever wasted being stressed over things I cannot control, and it also taught me the major importance of having a backup set of goggles. This I will take care of as soon as I get home.

A nice soak in the hot tub that I had all to myself, and a good night's sleep, can do wonders for a bad attitude; and a beautiful rainbow and friendly people can remind you of just how lucky you really are., Even if most of the day was a waste, you can always find a diamond or two hidden inside a bad day.

Day Fifty-Eight – Rawlins, Wyoming
(7/27/2017)

Today was a great day. We decided to head northwest. The landscape changed not far from the state line, lots of flat lands with small mountains in the far distance. The view was spectacular. The weather was perfect, hot sun and cool wind. I could not have asked for more. We stopped in a rest area to get some pictures and another bike pulled up. I started talking to the guy as he took his helmet off. He said he was heading to California from Colorado. The smile and pride in his voice was very electric. I doubt he was much over twenty (if that), and was traveling on his own. It was obvious that he was living his dream. I love to see a person's passion like that. As we get older, we learn to hide pure joy, like it is a bad thing. But kids have not learned this life lesson yet, and seeing it written all over his face was purely priceless.

The ride was awesome today. We did a lot of interstate riding, but with the lack of traffic, it was a little piece of heaven. In Wyoming, you can ride for many miles before a town pops up. They are few and far between (at least the part of Wyoming we have ridden in so far). Since it is in the plains, the wind is pretty strong. They have some pretty impressive wind farms. The one we passed will create enough electric for 24,756 homes. I know some think they are ugly, but I find them very beautiful.

I still have trouble trying to wrap my head around the massive amount of untouched land that we have in the US. The natural beauty is definitely something that we should all see at least once in our lifetime. Our national parks system is so very important to this generation and so many more that will come long after we are gone. I don't think I ever really understood the perfect beauty of the land until I saw it.

There are over 18 million acres of BLM- (Bureau of Land Management) administered public land in Wyoming. The BLM focuses on providing undeveloped recreation opportunities such as fishing, four-wheeling, sightseeing, river floating, hiking, and hunting. Although none of these are my passion (at least that I know of yet) I do enjoy riding through these lands, as Mother Nature is now my favorite artist and the canvas changes with every turn. She is much better than any virtual reality you will ever see.

Day Fifty-Nine – Cody, Wyoming
(7/28/2017)

Today was another beautiful day. We got up and packed and headed out down some of the most beautiful roads. We were told that we did not want to go to Wyoming, "there is nothing there," but I am so glad that we did come. Sometimes the nothing is just what the doctor ordered. It is like having the whole world all to ourselves. You can see the road laid out for miles while riding the plains and the mountains lay out in the background at least 50 miles away. The road is mainly straight, with a few wide slow curves every here and there. The scenery is ever changing; nothing is ever exactly as you have previously seen it. The only way I can describe it is that it was a perfect Zen kind of day, that perfect summer day that you never forget.

We stopped halfway here and had lunch in a little café next to a gas station. I had a pinwheel. It is a deep-fried cheese burger. I mean literally breaded and fried, totally not on my diet, but surprisingly good. I always ask the waitress what her favorite is when I go to a new restaurant; you can never go wrong this way. And when they suggest something I have never tried before, it becomes a must order.

We arrived in Cody, Wyoming around 6:00 p.m. There was a banner strung across the main street claiming there was a rodeo today. We pulled into the motel that I'd made the reservations for this morning, and there was a one-man band singing by the main office, and someone else giving kids horse rides around the pool area. There was also a pony taking a ride around the lot in a golf cart. I decided I totally love Cody, Wyoming.

After we checked in, we took a walk over to the rodeo. It turns out that they've had a rodeo every night in the summertime for the last sixty-five years. On the way over, Bonz said, "This isn't my first rodeo, you know. Well, actually, it is my first rodeo". It was so much fun. They had bucking broncos, barrel racing, calf roping and team roping, and, of course, there was also the bull riding. If you have never seen a rodeo, I highly suggest going the next time it is in your area.

It turns out that Cody is the home of Buffalo Bill, and the town revels in it. But unlike some towns, this one looks more like fun and less like a tourist trap. We definitely have some discovering to do around here. The room is adorable, with the wooden ceiling, and cedar closet, and all hardwood floors, and I am glad we are here for at least two days. This is going to be fun.

Day Sixty – Cody, Wyoming
(7/29/2017)

I slept late today. It was heavenly. We headed across the street and had a great breakfast. Since it was too late to head to Yellowstone, we decided to check out the town. We found lots of cute stores that sold the coolest things. Bonz picked up a new knife, and I ordered new cowboy boots. They make them to fit your feet! I had to stand in a box and leave my foot impressions and he measured my instep and calf. They should be home when I get there. I am pretty excited, as I have never had cowboy boot before, and these are very different. They have skulls and bones all over them, so buying them was a must.

We continued to check out more shops and met a few of the shop owners. Of course, the Harley Dealer was definitely one of the stops. This area is quite busy during the summer, but there is not much happening here when Yellowstone closes in the winter. Yellowstone is fifty-three miles from Cody, and they get hundreds of thousands of visitors each summer from all over the world. They have an amateur rodeo every night in the summer, and the town pretty much closes up at 8:00 when the rodeo starts.

We had dinner at the Irma Hotel. This is the hotel Buffalo Bill Cody owned when he started the town. It was named after his daughter Irma. The bar was the original bar he had handmade back in the 1900s. They even have a huge picture of what the hotel bar used to originally look like. Bonz kept looking for old bullet holes in the wall, but we did not see any.

Dinner was good and we have plans early tomorrow, so we came back to the motel and caught up on some reading. Today was a good day. Not too many miles, but lots of fun playing tourists.

Day Sixty-One – Cody, Wyoming
(7/30/2017)

We got up early today to head out to Yellowstone. We started our day at Grandma's Family Restaurant and had an excellent breakfast. The waitress made me look young, but the cup of coffee never hit empty. Alice was one of the best waitresses I have ever seen. She ran the place like the pro she is. With a start like this, you know it would be a great day.

Ten miles out of Cody is the largest tunnel in Wyoming. Not only is it one the largest, but there are three tunnels in a row, right by the dam. They are awesome to ride through on a motorcycle. The dam was built in 1902, with no steel reinforcements, and is still working today. When they built the dam, the town of Marquette was immersed in the Buffalo Bill Reservoir.

A few miles past the dam, you notice that most of the trees are dead. There are multiple mountains filled with dead pine tree bones. Half of them are standing and the other half have fallen. They leave the effect of many pickup sticks poured over the multiple mountains, half sticking straight up and the rest just poured over the landscape. The trees are the color of old barn wood, and we went quite a few miles before we saw any charring from a fire. There are multiple types of wildflowers growing on the floor of the forest now that the sun can reach them there, and quite a few small pine trees trying to fill the forest back in, through all the standing bones of the old pines. I guess riding through Yellowstone can really let you see the good, the bad, and the ugly when it comes to Mother Nature.

The park is huge, and I wish we had more time. We decided to see the geysers, as our other option was the canyons. We made it to Old Faithful ten minutes after it had gone off. The sky was turning black and the thunder and lightning was just starting its show. We had two options, try and outrun the storm, or wait it out. We decided it would be more fun to outrun it. We were mostly successful. About 10 miles from the dam, a huge wet blob hit my face shield. Told Bonz either a bird had just peed on me, or it was starting to rain. About thirty seconds later, it started to hail. Pellets of ice were pounding us while the huge drops of rain were intermittently hitting us. One minute later, it all stopped, so obviously it was not a bird. We were barely wet and the raindrops, though huge, were few and far between. Then the sky turned blue about five miles later, and the rest of the ride home was beautiful.

We saw many cool things in Yellowstone. A huge elk was feeding about ten feet from the road as we passed by. He ignored us. We also saw many small geysers, but none of them went off as we passed. There were bubbling mud pots and huge lakes, with beautiful blue water. We could have spent many days, as it would take that long just to see everything that is Yellowstone National Park, and even then, I am sure you would still have missed something. It is just that massive.

When we got back to Cody, we headed back to Grandma's Family Restaurant for another great meal, and headed to our temporary home for some much-needed sleep.

Day Sixty-Two – Billings, Montana
(7/31/2017)

We decided neither of us had ever been to Montana, so off we went to discover. The ride there was beautiful, and the road was fairly empty, but the landscape was awesome. The farmland looked prosperous; it is harvest time for the grain being grown. The bales of grain were piled high in the fields. Montana contains Glacier National Park, and portions of Yellowstone National Park, including three of the park's five entrances. Thirty-five percent of Montana's lands are administered by federal or state agencies.

As we were riding into Billings, we passed a Harley Dealer, Beartooth Harley Davidson, so we had to stop. I definitely needed a pin from Montana to add to our collection. Harley dealers are great places to meet other bikers who are traveling. We met a gentleman from the Smoky Mountains. He was having some work done on his bike before continuing on his trip. He was telling us about his run up Pike's Peak in Colorado. It is always fun discussing rides with other bikers.

We checked into our room early today and enjoyed a nice relaxing evening, ordering pizza to be delivered to our temporary home. Today was a good day. We will see what adventures tomorrow will bring.

Day Sixty-Three – Ranchester, Wyoming
(8/1/2017)

In Montana, there are tons of little casinos everywhere. We stopped for coffee and there was one connected to the convenience store. Bonz walked in to take a look. The gentleman that was working explained that there is no income tax because of the money that is raised from allowing gambling in the state. The law says that a business cannot have more than twenty machines, so all businesses have the machines in them. It was a cute little place and the man that was working was very nice, so we decided to make our donation. It took me longer than usual to lose, so that was fun.

We finished our coffee and headed out on our way. We saw a sign for the Little Big Horn battlefield, and decided we had to stop. The weather was in the 90s, so we took the bus tour. When I read about the battle in school, I assumed the mountains were bigger and that there were passes that they got caught in. (Or maybe it was Hollywood that left me with this impression). It is more like multiple rolling hills. We attacked the Indians for no reason at all other than greed. The plan was to capture the women and children and make them surrender to our will. We wanted their sacred land (the Black Hills) because there was gold in them there hills. They did not want to sell the land. So when we didn't get our way, we tried to take it.

Custer expected it to be easy to throw a surprise attack on the 500 Indians he was expecting. But there were 8000 at the camp. This was the greatest battle that the Lakota people had ever fought and won. But they definitely lost the war, and were forced back to the reservation. There are markers all over the rolling hills to mark the spot where people died. The white markers are for Custer's army and the brown markers show where the warriors fell. Many of the army is still buried there, but the Lakota people removed the warriors and reburied them as was their tradition. The only other American battle that is written about more than Little Big Horn is Gettysburg.

There is a national graveyard at Little Big Horn, like Arlington, where many soldiers from many wars are buried. Visiting an old battlefield is a little eerie. You can look over the fields and just imagine what was happening there where so many have died.

We left there about 6:00 p.m. and rode about 60 miles to the nearest motel. It was your average two-star motel, but it was loved. The rooms were clean, and there was a bar next door that served sloppy Joes or frozen pizza. We had the sloppy Joes and headed back to the room, where I promptly fell asleep until I was woken at midnight by a very loud windstorm. So I had to get out of bed to make sure the bikes were not blowing away.

When I woke up this morning, it was about 50 degrees out, a big change from the 90-degree day we had yesterday.

Day Sixty-Four – Moorcroft, Wyoming
(8/2/2017)

Today was a rough one. Woke up this morning and the temperature had dropped to about fifty degrees. By the time we had breakfast and got the bikes locked and loaded, the temperature had risen a little, but the sky was looking a little scary. We hit US 90, and the farther east we went, the stronger the wind got. The speed limit was 80 mph, but at one point as I was fighting the wind, I looked down and noticed I was only doing 55 mph (not a very safe speed when the limit is 80). Have you ever made a right turn while leaning left? It is an awkward turn on a major highway.

The wind was so strong that I could feel it pushing my tires out from under me, and both Bonz and I were riding at a sixty- to seventy-degree angle just to fight the wind and to go in a straight line down the highway. Being that I seem to have caught a case of trigger finger on my two middle fingers on my throttle hand (right hand) over the past two days, white knuckling it down the thruway was not helping it. Trigger finger is when you make a fist and then try to straighten your fingers and only some open up. The tendon on the offending fingers gets swollen from continuous use, and your fingers get stuck in a closed position. They snap open with a little extra help, but can be a little painful at times.

Riding down US 90 through Wyoming, there are these electronic signs to warn travelers about hazards ahead. All the signs were set to wish the bikers a safe ride to Sturgis. It was pretty cool. They said things like "Live 2 Ride, Ride 2 Live, Safe 2 Sturgis" and "Keep it vertical all the way to Sturgis; Watch for motorcycles". Most gas stations, motels, and restaurants have signs, "Bikers Welcome."

Having been in love with motorcycles for years and remembering the many years when the signs said the exact opposite, I found these signs very impressive. It is about time people quit hating other groups of people because they are a little different than them. If you only look for the bad in a group of people, that is all you will ever find. When you learn to accept people and their differences, you may find they are not really so very different from you after all. Don't get me wrong, there are bad people in every group, but that does not make all people in that group bad. This country is at each other's throats lately, and hating another group has become a new pastime. Everyone thinks their way is so superior, and I personally think both sides have valid points, and both sides have some off-the-wall thoughts too. Neither side is perfect. Until we stop vilifying groups and profiling people, we are all in trouble.

When we got to the motel, we met Ron, who was from Boston. He is on his way to Alaska on his BMW and had just left Sturgis. I have heard that Alaska is one of the most beautiful states, but it is way too cold in my book to be on my bucket list. I have learned to never say never, so at least for now, it is off the list of places I want to ride. But it is cool that he is living his dream. We only get one life; live it to the fullest. We enjoyed a nice dinner at the diner down the road with Ron and headed back to our temporary home for some much-needed rest for my hand.

Day Sixty-Five – Moorcroft, Wyoming
(8/3/2007)

Today was a productive day. The plan was to get the laundry done, as I have put it off as long as I could. We woke up late and headed to the diner for something to eat and some much-needed coffee. The laundromat was just down the street, and we were pleasantly surprised by the car wash that was connected to it. So when we left there, we not only left with clean clothes, we left with clean bikes too.

After we dropped our clothes off at our temporary home, we headed out to see Devil's Tower, or as the Lakota like to call it, Bear Lodge. It is a large formation of sedimentary rock that was formed fifty million years ago, and as the land eroded around it, the rock stayed in place. It kind of looks like a massive petrified tree trunk, and that can explain the Internet hoax I saw on Facebook stating that they found an old root system beneath it, claiming it was left by aliens. You have got to love the Internet.

Devil's Tower is our country's first national monument, proclaimed by Theodore Roosevelt in 1906 to protect it from commercial exploitation. The ride there is absolutely beautiful, as the mountains and the plains converge. You can see Devil's Tower from a distance as you ride around the wonderfully curvy road and you can see the canyon on your right, and the many phases in the life of the pines, burned in some spots and regrown in others, along the way.

Entering the park, there were a momma and two baby white-tailed deer playing in the field. One of the babies decided to race Bonz on his bike. Luckily for us, the momma pulled the baby back into the field before it came out into the street we were on. As we got to the base of the Tower, we could see the hawks flying in circles around the top of the tower. The information at the park said people climb this rock a lot, but we did not see any climbers at the time of our visit. On our way back out of the park, Bonz pulled over to show me the prairie dogs. I had never seen one before. They had a village at the beginning of the park, and they were everywhere. One dog kept barking at us as we took pictures. It sounded more like a squeak. I totally enjoyed watching them frolic around.

On our way out of the park, we had to stop at this little store. They had a billboard that said "Please stop, before we starve to death." It worked; we stopped. They had a small café there, so we had to order coffee and dessert, my favorite kind of dinner.

When we got back to the motel, I started packing so we can be ready in the morning for a new adventure. Yep, get up and do it again. Amen.

Assessing changes in our third quarter on the road:
Observations and speculations: (days 41-65)

So far this quarter we have been through Utah, Colorado, Wyoming, and Montana. Half of our time has been spent with friends from our HOG (Harley Owners Group) back home. We joined HOG last year when Bonz first retired. I was looking for a fun thing for us to do as a couple, and to find new people that enjoy the same things as us. Over the past thirty years, we have both worked separate shifts, so joining a group of any kind as a couple has never been an option for us before.

You find after two months together that there are subtle changes. For one, there is no stress, and it is so much easier to just be happy. Spending each and every day searching for "diamonds" gives you a renewed energy and zest for life. Our new goal is to learn how to just have fun, and we have been quite successful at this. Without complaining, the bad things that happen seem to dwindle down to nothing worth discussing and the good is all that is left. Bonz is a lot friendlier with strangers, and much more at ease with trying new things. Choosing a partner that you are compatible with is very important. I think our friendship has blossomed again and we do a lot more laughing than we used to. We are definitely working well as a team. Long-term travel takes you to different physical places around the world, but it also takes you to places in your mind you did not know existed. It changes the way you look at things and helps you realize what is important to you.

One thing I have truly noticed is how little we really need. Twice we have sent things home because the weight of carrying them is just not worth the effort. As Americans in a consumer culture, we have a tendency to buy things we really do not need. Back home I have a closetful of clothes and I don't really think I wear everything I own, and a house so full of things that I can't find them when I need them. Traveling with so little and not missing anything has changed my views on what is really necessary. My purse is small and can only carry the things I use every day. On this trip I have cleaned it out quite a bit. All the receipts and other things I have out there become more of a bother than necessary and seem to get in the way.

When traveling on a motorcycle, everything you carry must be necessary or gone. Breaking life down to a simple concept of need; we need food and shelter, and everything else is either a gift or an inconvenience. When you put life in this perspective, it simplifies many things. The three basics in life are now housing, food, and fun, and we have definitely done our part in spending on these three necessities.

The disbursement of funds for the third quarter of our trip was $950 on food, $1600 on lodging, $420 on gas, and $700 on incidentals, bringing our total this quarter to $3700.

Day Sixty-Six – Sturgis, South Dakota
(8/4/2017)

We woke up this morning and headed down to the gas station for some much-needed coffee. Things were bustling there, campers, cars, and bikes coming and going. Luckily, this station had a picnic table outside so we sat and drank our very large coffee while enjoying people watching. Had a nice talk with some guys from Chicago; they were leaving Sturgis and heading out to Cody to see the rodeo. We meet the nicest people on the road.

We headed back to the motel and packed up the bikes. We had a nice talk with one of the owners of the motel (The Moorcourt Motel). The owners are a young couple with a young beautiful daughter. I love to support family-owned businesses. It is so hard for small businesses to succeed; I hope they can make their dreams come true with this adorable motel.

Our first stop was the Deluxe Harley Davidson of Sundance. We picked up a pin from there, and hung out for a little bit. There were bikes parked up and down the street. I guess we are not the only ones that think a dealership is a tourist attraction.

We hopped back on US 90 and headed east to Sturgis. The ride was much nicer today, as the wind was much more manageable than the other day. We found the No Name City campground, where we had reserved a cabin, and checked in. The cabin is extremely nice. It has a porch outside with chairs, and the inside is all knotty pine, with hardwood floors, a bed, a couch, a table, chairs, and most importantly, a coffee pot, and a TV for Bonz. It also has a microwave and small refrigerator. The one thing it does not have is a bathroom, but the showers and bathrooms are not far at all.

It was time to eat, so we headed into town to see what was going on. When we got off the exit for town, we found a cute little restaurant, Jam Bonz, and the food was very good. Bonz had linguini with chicken gumbo, and I had a burger. We definitely left full. We decided to get our bearings and headed to Main Street. They have it blocked off to all traffic except bikes, and there were five or six blocks of bikes parked four across, leaving two small paths to ride down to try to find a spot.

The streets were full of people and energy. There was a band playing, so we stopped and watched them for a while. This is only the first day of Bike Week, and usually it is the slowest day, as people are still arriving. I think our timing for this was perfect, as we are ready for a little crazy after two months on the road. After walking around downtown for a while, we hit the grocery store for some … you guessed it … Coffee, before we headed back to the cabin.

Sitting on my little porch and watching all the bikes riding up and down US 90 is very relaxing to me. When the sun is up, you can see the beautiful works of art pass by like my own personal parade, and at night you can see the lights and hear the roar of the engines. I could do this forever! I'm so excited to be here; let's see what tomorrow will bring …

Day Sixty-Seven – Sturgis, South Dakota
(8/5/2017)

Well, my coffee pods I bought did not fit the coffee pot that came with the cabin … Don't make my brain work without coffee. I walked outside and everyone was walking around with coffee. Turns out they sell breakfast and coffee in the bar area at the campground. Life is good again! After enjoying our libation, Bonz came up with the great idea of tying the coffee from the pods into a coffee filter, so problem solved for tomorrow. Now all we need are real coffee mugs and life will be perfect again.

After breakfast, we headed out to the Full Throttle Saloon. It is the world's largest biker bar. It is a 600-acre indoor/outdoor bar that has 300 employees, and is only open for the rally. There are cabins you can rent and a campground on the premises. There is a huge outdoor stage, and small vendor buildings running up the sides. I did pick up a few coffee mugs for morning while we were there. The bar is massive, and decorated in metal. There are punch presses and other large metal machines decorating the bar. There is a huge metal sculpture of a man on a motorcycle holding a chainsaw out in front of the bar. The sculpture is depicting Jessie James Dupree, lead singer in Jackyl, and part owner of the bar. We see Jackyl every year at Ohio Bike week, and he can play a mean chainsaw.

There is more to this bar than I can even think to describe. It is definitely the world's largest biker bar. There is a lot of construction still going on, as there was a fire in 2015 that burned the original bar to the ground. Rumor has it, it used to be very impressive before the fire. The bar is being rebuilt in a new location, but I was pretty impressed with how much is already there.

Bonz was getting hungry, so we decided to head back to town, and the insanity that is the Sturgis Bike Rally. David Allen Coe was playing at the Iron Horse saloon, so after finding a place to park (easier said than done), we headed over there and had lunch before the concert. He was absolutely fabulous! At 73 years old, he has not lost any of his charm. I have been a fan of his since the 70s, when you had to order his albums by mail, from the back of the Easyriders magazines, because they were not sold is stores. He is the original outlaw country singer and has had a huge hand in making country music what it is today. Without him, it would still be the old twang it used to be. I am so blessed to have seen him perform live.

After the concert, we walked around town and had fun people watching. People are so funny sometimes, and not even trying to be. One guy had a four-foot helmet on as he rode by on his bike. Another good-looking older biker had the perfect biker look, shredded jeans, combination dreadlocks and braids in his long gray hair, kidney belt over his T-shirt; can't explain it, but he had the look down perfectly and it worked for him. He was standing next to Bonz, and we were enjoying the looks and reactions he was getting. The guys would look him up and down, and the girls would ask to get their picture with him. Bonz told him he should charge for a picture. (I think he is a little upset that the showgirls in Vegas get paid for pictures, and men in Sturgis don't). There were also the usual girls running around in paint instead of shirts, and the chicks arguing over who was more hammered, while their old men just rolled their eyes; but mostly there were just a lot of bikers walking around that were excited to be there, so everyone was in a very good mood, and very friendly.

Bonz is having a lot of fun in Sturgis. After pulling him away from home for the past two months, I think he is getting a little homesick. He said it is nice to have a little insanity back in our lives. After hanging out with me for the past 30 years, I think he is now appreciating all the insanity that is our regular life. At least our life is never dull. It is funny what people miss when they are away from home for a while.

Day Sixty-Eight – Sturgis, South Dakota
(8/6/2017)

Mmmm, coffee. Life is good. Coffee on the deck; visiting with all my neighbors. Life is better than good. Life is great! Getting ideas of which roads are the best, and what is worth making a trip to and what is not: priceless. After showers, we headed out to Mount Rushmore. We rode through a cute little town called Keystone. There were bikes parked everywhere, so we decided to stop and see what was up. After a nice walk through town, we headed out to find the faces in the mountain.

Looking at Mt. Rushmore, I find it hard to believe that it only took fourteen years to create this huge sculpture. Work on the mountain ended in 1941, when WWII broke out. Originally, the four faces would also get busts, and there were supposed to be stairs up the mountain to a national document archive. The cave for the national document archive was started but never fully finished. The thought was that there is very little information on how and why the pyramids and Sphinx where built, and they did not want this to happen in the future to Mt Rushmore.

There is an amphitheater built in front of Mt. Rushmore. A $56 million redevelopment was completed in 1998. with the addition of a new parking structure, amphitheater, museum/theater complex, Visitor Orientation Center, Presidential Trail, gift shop, bookstore, and dining facilities. Because of this they claim there is no fee to enter the park, but there is a $10 per vehicle charge to park, and the national park pass does not cover this fee. We were there during the day, so we did not get to see the lightshow they have every night, when they light up the faces in the mountain. I do hear it is spectacular.

Since there are many motorcycles visiting Mt. Rushmore during the rally at Sturgis, they send all the motorcycles to the ground floor of the parking area. They send them out a one-way with cones set up. This is usually a one-way (going in), and there are cones set up with a stop sign not placed very well. As a matter of fact, it was facing the wrong way, and I never saw it. Bonz did, but did not think it was set up for us since the cones were there and the lane was usually set for cars going in the other direction.

There were also four state police sitting right after the badly-placed stop sign; motorcycle profiling at its finest. We were pulled over and questioned on the last drink we had and if we were carrying any drugs on our person or on our bikes. Bonz stated he does not drink, and I stated I have not had any alcohol or drugs in 20 years, and I guaranteed there was nothing illegal on my bike. He let us go with a warning. I detest motorcycle profiling, and this was blatant. Some states have passed laws to illegalize this unconstitutional practice, but I guess it is still being used in South Dakota.

Crazy Horse was our next stop. It is about seventeen miles away from Mt. Rushmore. It is not a national park, so I had no problem spending the five-dollar per person entrance fee. It is still in the process of being built, and truly impressive. The Black Hills are very special to the Indian people, and they decided that if the American people could carve their presidents in the mountain, they wanted one of their legends carved in the mountain too. The entire four faces in Mt. Rushmore can fit inside the head of Crazy Horse, just so you can imagine the size of this project.

The mission of Crazy Horse Memorial Foundation is to protect and preserve the culture, tradition, and living heritage of the North American Indians. Crazy Horse is funded by the income that comes from visitors and private donations, and is not in any way federally funded. The income from visitors helps to fund the work still being done on the sculpture, and hopes to establish and operate the Indian University of North America, and when practical, a medical training center for American Indians. There is a great need for medical help on most of the reservations today. I was very impressed with Crazy Horse, and would highly recommend a trip to the information center there.

 We originally were going to head to Deadwood, but it was getting late, so we stopped at a bar and grill connected to a gas station and grabbed something to eat before we headed back to camp. The food was good, and we decided to see Deadwood on another day.

Day Sixty-Nine – Sturgis, South Dakota
(8/7/2017)

Had a fun-filled day of nothing today. We took the day off. Bonz enjoyed a nap, and we hung around the campground for most of the day.

Talk around camp is to ride safe; the police have successfully pulled over about 50% of the campers over so far; searched a quite few bikes; harassed people waiting for Da Bus; and DWIs are already up 18% from last year at this time; and it's only Monday. It is a shame that they feel the need to harass anyone on two wheels, when all we are doing is dumping lots of money into the area to begin with. The local police are friendly, but the rent-a-cops they imported for this event are trying to make a name for themselves, and rumor has it, their pay is in accordance with the amount of tickets written. Everyone here knows if you're going to drink, you better take Da Bus, as they run from all the campgrounds to the downtown area.

While sitting around the campfire last night, some of the guys were discussing a new campground just one exit down, named Kickstands. They have bands and a lot of things going on all day long. I think the big attraction today was that they are right off the next exit, and no traffic to fight. So we decided to head over and check it out. The bar area was absolutely beautiful; they had just finished remodeling it. It was done in old barn wood. They were serving spaghetti, and that is Bonz's favorite. So we stayed for dinner and to watch the bike rodeo. They are always fun.

They had the usual things like the drunken bartender, where the driver has to weave through the cones while the passenger holds a tray of drinks and tries not to spill them. And the old hotdog on a string, where the passenger has to bite as much of the hotdog off as they ride under it, and my favorite to watch, the slow race, last one in wins. They also had a bike show with trophies, tallest apes, largest belly, etc. It was lots of fun.

After dinner, we headed back to camp to finish our do-nothing day, and enjoyed some reading. Sometimes it is just more fun to take a day off and do nothing. Seems there is always too much going on for this to be an option at home.

Day Seventy – Sturgis, South Dakota
(8/8/2017)

Today was a fun day. We took a ride out to Deadwood. Deadwood is an old mining town built by the Chinese. Rumor has it, there were tunnels built so the Chinese could get around at night. It was legal to shoot Chinese after dark in Deadwood, back in the day. Our history is so weird sometimes. When gold was found in the Black Hills in 1874, practically overnight, the tiny gold camp boomed into a town that played by its own rules that attracted outlaws, gamblers, and gunslingers, along with the gold seekers. Wild Bill Hickok and Calamity Jane were just a few that lived here. In 1989, limited-wage gambling was legalized and Deadwood was reborn, before becoming just another ghost town.

Today it has casinos, bars, restaurants, and cute boutiques (which also have bars in them). It is a little strange to walk into a woman's clothing store and see a bar in the back of it, but this is commonplace in Deadwood. Of course, being Bike Week, the streets are lined with Harley's and there are many people wandering the streets, as this is on almost everyone's to-do list during Sturgis. We stopped at one of the bars and had meatball subs and watched this Willy Nelson (kind of) lookalike musician/comedian for a while. He was pretty funny. The sky was turning pretty black, so we decided to head back to Sturgis and do some more people watching. This is always interesting. There were still the girls with the painted tops, and today we saw a bride and groom ride by. They looked quite happy. Her dress looked more like something I would put on a three year old, but each to their own.

We decided today would be a good day to go bar hopping. So we checked out quite a few of the bars on Main Street. We started out at One Eyed Jack's, and then just hit bars that had bands playing. That was a lot of fun; we saw a bunch of different bands play today. Some had the whole crowd getting rowdy, and others had a much mellower crowd, but all the music was good. Today was a really fun day.

Day Seventy-One – Sturgis, South Dakota
(8/9/2017)

The thing about Sturgis, South Dakota, is that fall weather comes earlier than it does in NY. I think of August as the hottest month of the year. The weather has been around the mid-70s during the day, but the weather drops considerably at night. Right now, it is 61 degrees and expected to drop to 52 tonight. The wind picks up a lot here too; some days are not bad, but there are the days the wind enjoys slapping you around a bit. Luckily, it has not gotten as bad as it was riding in.

The nice thing about the cooler weather is that you can comfortably wear all the cool leather and not melt, and wearing a coat is a lot more fun in the fall then it is in the winter. The problem is that fall is here a lot sooner than I am used to, so I keep forgetting to pack warm clothes in the saddle bags. I keep thinking that I will be fine with just a hoodie. Those cute young girls with their painted-on shirts have got to be freezing at night in town.

We have met so many nice people in Sturgis; it is amazing when you think about it. Half a million people from all over the world migrate to Sturgis once a year for this rally. I have seen people waring patches from Norway, Canada, South Africa, and just about every state in the US. I have seen bikes from little scooters to custom jobs costing more than my house. There are people here from all walks of life; we have met retired police, retired people, and nurses that work in jails, to CEOs. The one thing we have not seen here are arguments and fights. When we've struck up a conversation with someone, they have all been nice, some even funny. Many people have luxury RVs set up, but a lot of people have tents too. One guy even has a pop-up trailer he tows behind his bike. (Surprised I have only seen one.)

You feel welcome wherever you go (excluding Mt Rushmore). This place is peaceful and fun, with a non-judgmental attitude of the people attending. I think one girl I was talking to summed it up perfectly. I asked her, "How are you doing?" and she answered, "Just so very glad to be here." And that is exactly what Sturgis is all about. It is the yearly pilgrimage of bikers to Sturgis from all over the world that are all just happy to be here. The air is filled with the sound of motorcycles rumbling twenty-four/seven in the background, with laughter in the forecourt.

People are nice and respectful to each other, and the streets are blocked off so only bikes can ride down Main Street. Cars are forbidden; pedestrians yield the right of way to motorcycles; and it is one of the few places that you will see chivalry is not dead. One thing about a biker and his lady is that they are treated like gold (despite the rumors). Once you get past the clothing (or lack of) and watch the dance, you can see the love and respect between them. Biker chicks are treated like gold, as they should be, but in return they make sure their men are taken care of. It's a quiet dance, but if you watch quietly you can still see the waltz.

We did not do much today, just headed east away from the mayhem to get a decent meal. You can buy many things at a great price in Sturgis, like leather and other vendor offerings, but food and drinks seem to be sold at top dollar. We found a nice quiet biker bar on an access road that served food and had a nice meal, before heading to the grocery store for some breakfast items for mornings. After tying down the groceries to get them back to camp, we headed home for a nice quiet day.

Day Seventy-Two – Sturgis, South Dakota
(8/10/2017)

Today was a fun-filled day of crazy. We went down town to find the pin stop. Usually, this is one of our first things to do, but we were having too much fun, and the pin stop closes at 5:00 p.m. Every time we remember, it is after 5:00. We found a nice area to park, same as the other day, at the far end of Main Street. After parking we watched the tow truck pick up three bikes that parked in front of the yellow curb. If you like your bike, don't park in front of the yellow curb while in Sturgis.

While wandering around looking for the pin stop, we passed a vendor who had many items with fringe, and anyone that knows me knows I am a fringe nut. They even had saddle bags with fringe! So, of course, I had to buy some. He also offered to sew fringe in a pair of new chaps, so I had to buy those too. It is getting harder and harder to find new fringe for my motorcycle, so when you see it, you have to buy it. Hey, fringe makes me happy, what can I say? It's cheaper than diamonds, so that makes Bonz happy, so that makes it a win-win situation.

After grabbing something for Bonz to eat and picking up our HOG pins, we sat back in our favorite rocking chair in front of The Iron Horse Saloon, and had a great chat with brother Speed. He has been working security there for over 10 years, and is definitely an old-school biker, who has owned the same scooter since 1970. He has ridden that bike all over the world, and on more than one occasion played a part in a movie. We enjoyed listening to his tales of the road, and how different things were riding a motorcycle with a 1% club back in the 70s. He did not give us his exact age, but from the stories he told I would guess he was in his later 70s, and still living the dream, still riding all over the United States. What a gift and a pleasure it was to meet him.

The chaps were finished, and Bonz installed my new bags on my bike, and man, they look sharp. So back to camp we went, before I could shop some more. Our neighbors a few cabins down decided to go to the Bikers' Ball with us at the Full Throttle Saloon (FTS). Remember, it's the largest biker bar in the world. On Thursday night, during The Sturgis Rally, they have the Bikers' Ball. Two bands play, one inside, and Jackyl on the large outside stage. There are quite a few bars setup, and one even has a stripper pole at each corner and many girls dancing the poles on top of the bar.

The store was still open, and the place was packed. I even saw a girl putting on a flame-spinning show, and she ate the fire. The thing about it being the largest biker bar in the world, and being packed, is you still have lots of elbow room, and we even found some chairs. We decided to take Da Bus to the FTS, so there would be no issues getting home. Da Bus has disco lights and music playing, and sells beer and water on the bus. They even handout markers so you can sign your name on the ceiling or wall, wherever you desire. Our driver to the FTS was even dressed like Santa Claus.

The inside band was playing country music and Bonz even asked me to dance, and Tarah and I also danced. We headed outside to hear Jackyl play (remember, during Ohio Bike Week, he was the one that played a mean chainsaw). It was fun. After the show, we headed out to catch Da Bus. We had to change buses three times to get back to our campsite. The first bus was standing room only, and the second bus had a lot more elbow room. As we got off the second bus, the third and final bus was ready and waiting for us. We (luckily) sat in the back of the bus.

When the driver got on, he was wearing a baby blue Speedo under his chaps, and the music was blaring. Everyone on the bus was singing to the tunes, and a few were even dancing. The girl with the painted-on shirt put on a nice pole dance for the boys on Da Bus. The beer was still being sold for the trip, and it did not look as though some needed any more. Right before our stop (which was the first stop), the driver pulled the bus over to the side of the road to really give us a show. He was stripping off his shirt and scarves, and even gave a few of the ladies sitting in the front of the bus an unexpected lap dance. Thank God, the Speedo stayed on. It was pretty funny. It was all done in fun, and taken that way, but definitely one of the most fun bus rides I have ever been on.

Dave, our neighbor, said, "Can you imagine taking this bus to work in the morning?" And the truth is, things like this are always more fun, and better received, around last call. Yes, today definitely was a fun-filled day of crazy.

Day Seventy-Three – Sturgis, South Dakota
(8/11/2017)

We rode up to Leads, South Dakota, to meet Darla and Dave. They worked with Bonz before his retirement, and he had not seen them in over a year. It was fun. We met them at Louie's, which, by the way, has the best burgers! The ride up there through Deadwood was nice. The ride was all rolling turns and not too many cars. Hey, it's Rally Week. Of course, there were many bikes, but that's the point.

As soon as we got there, it started to sprinkle. We had a table outside, and moved under the roof cover halfway through lunch as the sky decided to open up. After we finished lunch it was still raining, so we moved inside as the temperature dropped and all our coats were still tied to the back of the bike. Our timing was perfect for lunch, as we just had more time to visit.

As I am learning, in the mountains the rain never stays for very long, and the sun came back out by the time we were ready to leave. We enjoyed a nice ride back, and decided to stay in tonight as it was pretty chilly after the rain. We had planned on doing laundry (our one job) but watching a movie seemed to take precedence. Funny how the less you have to do, the more you put it off. No worries; tomorrow is another day.

Day Seventy-Four – Sturgis, South Dakota
(8/12/2017)

We headed into town for the last night of festivities. Main Street was a lot less busy than it has been; this was obvious by the empty parking spaces on Main. There had not been any of those all week. Being that people come from all over the country to enjoy the Rally, I am assuming many have to be back to work on Monday. Many Sturgis businesses are open just for the Rally, Full Throttle being one. One-Eyed Jacks (casino and bar/restaurant) is only open for 11 weeks of the year, closing after the crowd leaves from the Rally. Many of the other businesses go back to what they usually are, that not being leather shops and biker T-shirt shops. The population of Sturgis is a little over 6,000 people during the rest of the year. Not enough people to keep businesses running all year.

Being that the Rally was still going on and there were still thousands of people there, we enjoyed people watching and a nice dinner on Main Street. We also stopped to watch a band. There was something sad about the last night at the Rally. Coming back to the camp, many people had left already. But 40 people from Europe did come in and fill our campground back up again. They had rented Harleys in Chicago and were traveling the US for three weeks; pretty cool. I love to hear people who are living their dreams.

When we got back, Bonz bought me an ice cream at the bar at the campsite and we sat at the firepit and met more people. One guy from Ohio had been on the road since January first. He definitely had us beat.

Everyone has a story, and I love to listen to bikers tell stories. They always have just the right amount of crazy to keep you laughing.

Day Seventy-Five – Wall, South Dakota
(8/13/2017)

Well, the plan today was to be lazy and work on securing my new saddlebags, see if I could fix the issue we were having with the microphone on my Scala Rider (helmet communication device), and get some laundry done. I was smoking a cigarette on the porch when the owner came by and asked if we were leaving today. I had thought the cabin was paid until Monday. Well, after checking our reservation, I realized we were supposed to be out today. That left us a half hour to get packed up. Good thing we are now pros at getting locked and loaded. We set the GPS to the Badlands National Park and headed out.

The weather was perfect, and it felt great to be back on the road and off wandering again. We stopped for gas and met a nice group of BACA Bikers (BACA = Bikers Against Child Abuse). When I saw the patch, I had to go and thank them for their service. If you have never heard about them, you should Google it. Being that my soft spot in life is children, and their main focus is protecting the children that have been wounded or abused, I have a lot of respect for them. They are the keepers of the children.

We found an IHOP along the way and decided to stop to feed Bonz, since it was past noon. Breakfast was good and we left full. When I put my helmet back on, I could not get the microphone to work on my helmet. I could hear Bonz, but he could not hear me. The wire had been giving us issues, so we found a Lowe's nearby and tried taping it with some duct tape, because everyone knows duct tape can fix almost anything. After a good forty-five minutes of messing with the tape I finally got it working again.

It was a little weird riding down US 90 with so many cars, and so few bikes on it. The past nine days, it has been the complete opposite. We saw a rest area right before the turn off for the Badlands National Park, and decided to stop to pee, because all that coffee we drank will go right through a person. When we put the helmets back on, the wire would not re-connect. I tried re-taping it, but no. Then I unpacked the super glue and tried to strengthen the connection with the glue. I thought it was going to work, but when I put the helmet back on, the wire came off the other end. So I successfully spent most of the day trying to get this stupid wire to work and successfully made sure it never would again.

We decided to quit for the day and see if we could find a place that sells the Scala Rider so we could get another microphone piece, as we were now completely spoiled with the ability to communicate while riding. No worries, nearest Yamaha dealer was only 250 miles away. Too bad Harley is not selling the Scala line; it was five miles away.

We hit the local Dairy Queen, because it is a known fact that ice cream can make you feel better when things don't go the way you want them to. And my Blizzard was awesome, so all is right with the world again.

Day Seventy-Six – Kennebec, South Dakota
(8/14/2017)

After breakfast, we were locked and loaded and headed to the Badlands. First, we stopped at the Badlands Harley Dealer for a pin. Across the street was the world-famous Wall Drugs. Wall Drugs became world famous by putting out signs for free ice water. Yep, water made them famous. In 1936, while building Mt. Rushmore was in process, Dorothy Husted came up with an idea of putting signs on the 16A for free ice water for the weary travelers driving down the hot prairie. The signs worked immediately. They ran out of ice the first day and today, Wall Drugs takes up most of the block. It is a must-stop on your way down Route 90. There are billboards for miles letting you know you are getting close. The store is actually pretty cool. It now has a little bit of everything. The first café entrance goes to the "Mall." It is set up like an old west town (inside Wall Drugs). It has many cute storefronts, but no walls separating the sections. If you ever pass Wall, South Dakota, be sure to save time to check this adorable shop out.

After we left Wall, we headed to the Badlands National Park; it was less than eight miles away. Having no microphone on my helmet and the GPS on my bike, I had to wear Bonz's helmet. This was the first time I had ever worn a full-face helmet, and hopefully the last time. Have you ever played that game when you were young and squished your cheeks together to make a fish face? Yep, that was me in Bonz's helmet. But I could talk to him and let him know which way to turn, to find the park.

The Badlands National Park was another awesome virtual reality game. The park starts with prairie grass everywhere. We passed some mountain goats and more prairie dogs. Then, all of a sudden, the prairie grass disappears and the canyons open up in the ground. The ride is absolutely beautiful. We got halfway through the park, and traffic was stopped and there were EMTs and ambulances around a little blue car. We were at an overlook, so we pulled in and parked, as it did not look like we would be moving anytime soon. A little while later, a helicopter showed up to take the person to the hospital. At first, we thought someone might have fallen in the canyon, but it turns out someone had a possible heart attack. Their ability to help someone in the middle of nowhere was very impressive.

After the helicopter flew off for a hospital, the road was opened again for traffic. There is only one paved road in the Badlands National Park. We wound down the beautiful winding road and enjoyed the sharp sandblasted mountain tops, and beautiful canyons sprinkled with flat prairie. The ride was awesome. The weather was awesome, and the road was just perfect with all the twisties and beautiful scenery. A girl could not ask for a more perfect day. The park also is the home of the world's richest fossil bed, dating back as far as 33.9 million to 23 million years old. There is even a sign asking you not to remove any fossils. Bonz liked that sign, but was not happy with all the rattlesnake warning signs.

We stopped in the park at the little café they have and had lunch, and the price was actually reasonable. I think this is the first national park that we have found with reasonable food prices. Not only were the prices for a meal good, the food was good too. We left very happy.

We headed back down 90 East where the towns are few and far between. South Dakota is really a beautiful state. The wind was there, as it always is in South Dakota, but it was not undoable. We found a cheap motel and decided to quit for the night after picking up a handful of junk food in case my Bonz gets hungry during the night. Have to keep the Bonz fed. Happy man, happy life.

Day Seventy-Seven – Sioux Falls, South Dakota
(8/15/2017)

The weather was a little chilly today. Definitely a chaps and coat kind of day. We headed out back down US 90 East. Nice crisp ride. The black skies were following us the whole way, but luckily, the rain stayed behind us. We stopped at a rest area in Chamberlain, where Dignity was installed on September 17, 2016. Dignity is a 50-foot tall stainless-steel statue installed in Chamberlain along the banks of the Missouri River. Dignity depicts a young Native American woman receiving a star quilt. It was created by Dale Claude Lamphere.

According to the artist, "*Dignity* represents the courage, perseverance, and wisdom of the Lakota and Dakota culture in South Dakota. My hope is that the sculpture might serve as a symbol of respect and promise for the future. *Wind and sun will pass through the sculpture so that rather than resisting the natural environment, she moves with it. She is of the earth and sky and the water that surround her.*"

The piece is utterly stunning, and my words are not good enough to describe her beauty.

We stopped in Mitchell for lunch at Hardy's, and were going to visit the Corn Palace two miles away, but the clouds were moving in on us so we decided seeing the only corn palace in the world was not really worth getting wet for. According to their website, "The Corn Palace is decorated with several murals made out of 10 different colors of corn, each framed with native grasses, straw, milo, and sour dock. A local farmer grows all the corn for the Palace. A local artist designs the murals, and a team of approximately 20 workers change out the murals every year beginning in late-August and working into September (as crops become available). The Palace is never un-decorated, as the murals are not taken down until it is time to replace them in the late summer, when the work is a gradual process." (http://visitmitchell.com/attractions-posts/worlds-only-corn-palace/) There. Now you know as much about it as I do, so when you visit this unique palace, please let me know what you think of it.

When we got to Sioux Falls, we decided to quit for the day and get some laundry done. We had already pushed this necessary evil to its limits. Any longer and I would have been riding down the road in my chaps and swim suit. This may be a good look for some, but it would not be a good look for me. Just as we pulled up to the Day's Inn, the rain decided to fall. Our timing could not have been better. And luckily for all the truck drivers out there, the Day's Inn has customer laundry on site.

Day Seventy-Eight – Sioux Falls, South Dakota
(8/16/2017)

We woke up this morning and it was raining. Got up and went to breakfast and it was still raining. We took a shower and the rain got even harder. So we did what any self-respecting bad ass biker with time would do. We rented the room for another day to wait out the rain.

Hotels can be a little boring, and daytime TV sucks, so I grabbed my book and found a comfy chair and read for a while, while Bonz took a nap. For some reason, he still thinks I snore, but we all know he is wrong on that account. We ordered pizza because the rain never quit, and enjoyed a day of accomplishing absolutely nothing. Sometimes this is a fun thing to do.

Day Seventy-Nine – La Crosse, Wisconsin
(8/17/2017)

Well, we rode through three states today. Started in South Dakota, rode through Minnesota, and landed in Wisconsin. Most of the day was spent in Minnesota. At least three-quarters of US 90 in Minnesota is under construction, and the other quarter should be. It was like riding on a rocking horse. There are patches on top of patches on their roads.

The temperature never made it to 70 degrees, and the wind thought we were there as an Uke, in a fun new Aikido move. (That is the person who "receives" a technique, so the other guy can practice his moves). First it would push you from the right for a while, then it would try to knock you off balance by whipping around and slapping you on the left with no notice it was changing direction. Aikido is all built on circles, and off-balance points. Luckily for us, we were not very good Ukes, as we kept our balance and our tires on the road. But the wind was successful in sucking out all our energy by the time we quit for the day.

At a gas stop, we ran into a couple from Florida, whom we had met two days ago at a rest stop in South Dakota. They were on a kick-ass red custom-to-the-max trike. (Definitely not one you would forget). He had done all the work himself. I love to see people's talents when it comes to things they love. We stopped to chat, and another five bikes pulled up. Seems everyone but us got caught in the rain. Our timing must have just been good today, or Mom is making sure the angels in charge of the rain are watching over us, which is quite possible as I do believe God rides a Harley.

We stopped for lunch at an Applebee's and lucky for us, there was a Harley Dealership not far from the restaurant. Of course, it was mandatory to stop and grab a pin from Bergdale Harley Davidson, as any respecting Harley owner knows that Harley dealerships are a must-visit on a trip. Some of the best tourist attractions are the dealerships. There are always other bikers milling around, and great places to visit and meet new people and get the goods on great rides in the area. We had some fun exchanging giggles at Bonz's expense, which is always fun. He just did not understand the phrase "not shopping," as I paid for my merchandise. It is kind of on the same line as not snoring ...

Well, time for a well-deserved nap so we can get up and do it again. Amen.

Day Eighty – Janesville, Wisconsin
(8/18/2017)

The weather was just perfect today, and the wind was minimal. It made for a perfect ride. Not very far to go today, so we took our time. We stopped for gas and lunch around Madison at The Iron Skillet and enjoyed a very nice buffet.

We found my sister Karen's house and the battery was dead on her garage door opener, so we made ourselves comfortable on her front porch while waiting for her to get home from work. I texted her and told her that either the battery was dead or we were at the wrong house. Either way, we were making ourselves comfortable and would find out which when she got home. No worries for us; it was a beautiful day and there was an electrical outlet on the porch.

Luckily for us, the battery was dead, and we were at the right house. We headed out to dinner and Phil joined us. The Food at Fredrick's supper club in Milton was wonderful, and the company was even better. After staying up talking most of the night, I crashed on the most comfortable bed. What a perfect day this turned out to be.

Day Eighty-One – Janesville, Wisconsin
(8/19/2017)

It was another beautiful day. I slept in till 8:00 and everyone else was up by then. Bonz was getting ready to head out with Phil, who was coaching fourth/fifth grade football in Madison, so they were going to be gone for the day. We'd had the parts for my helmet sent to Karen's house after I successfully totaled the microphone the other day. The guys at Canandaigua Motorsports were so awesome, and got the parts out the day I called, so everything was here when we arrived. The new parts are even better than the old ones. No small wire on this one for me to break! Yeah, no more squishy fishy face from wearing Bonz's full-face helmet anymore! Karen and I headed out to do some serious garage sale shopping before we hit the grocery store. Found some great treasures in our travels. And treasure hunting is always fun.

As we were checking out at the grocery store, my other sister Lyn and her husband Bart called and they were at the house, so off we went to join them. After visiting awhile, we headed into downtown Janesville, to the Bodacious Block. We had lunch at the Bodacious So Chop, a great salad café, right next to the Bodacious Olive, a cute oil shop, for cooking oils. We went to the Bodacious Cupcake for dessert, but they were all sold out for the day. I guess their cupcakes are awesome.

After we got back, Bonz and Phil joined us and the boys made an awesome dinner of steak, corn on the cob, and bread, and we finished off the night at the firepit in Karen and Phil's backyard. It was a fun day with family. I just wish we all lived closer so we could do this more often.

Day Eighty-Two – Janesville, Wisconsin
(8/20/2017)

Another fun-filled day with family. Phil got up and made biscuits and gravy for everyone, and Karen and Phil's son, Chris, came over to visit. We packed up some furniture and Karen, Lyn, and I followed Chris and his friend in the truck to Chris's new apartment in Madison. His new apartment is so much nicer than most college off-campus apartments I have seen. It's a large, beautiful four-bedroom apartment that had clean dishes and furniture by the time we left. Of course, my sisters and I all take credit for this as Chris and his friends did all the bull work.

Phil kept the boys busy with projects, hanging pictures and TVs, and verifying the TV was hung correctly by watching pre-season football on it. We enjoyed another awesome dinner with family when we got back from Madison. It is always good to play catch up, as we never get enough family time, with so many miles between us. We did successfully book a house for next year's vacation; hey, we need something to look forward to!

My right hand is still giving me a lot of issues, so a day not working the throttle is very good for it. Karen let me use some of her tiger balm and it seems to be helping a lot. tiger balm is from China and has been around since the 1870s. Basically, it is a menthol rub. And its side effect is that it will definitely clear your sinuses, and the sinuses of anyone sitting anywhere near you. But it makes my hand hurt less, so healthy sinuses to all.

Lyn and Bart headed back to Chicago, and Karen, Phil, Bonz, and I settled in to watch a movie before we retired for the evening. Weekends just seem to whip by, especially when you are totally enjoying yourself.

Day Eighty-Three – Janesville, Wisconsin
(8/22/2017)

The eclipse was today. People traveled all over this country to watch the totality. Complete darkness during the day when the moon covered the sun. It was a little cloudy today, and we did notice the darkening of the sun, but we watched the eclipse on TV. I decided that I like my eyes. They are not perfect, but neither am I, but they work, and I prefer to keep them working as long as possible.

So what to do during an eclipse? Go shopping, of course! So, off we went to the local Harley dealer in Janesville, Boardtracker Harley Davidson. We picked up a pin and some oil for the bikes. We unsuccessfully tried to talk Phil into buying a new bike, but since he just bought a new house, he decided to wait on that purchase. So off we went to eat.

We stopped at a nice Irish bar for lunch. Food was good, and service was great, so we left happy. Next we headed to Home Depot to pick up a few things. I lost the boys, so I texted Bonz that I was out front, but that did not help as he did not have his phone on him. I called Phil about twenty minutes later and they quit searching the store for me and joined me out front. (What I really meant when I said searching the store was that they quit shopping and joined me out front).

We got back to the house and promptly took a nap until Karen got home from work and we all headed out to a wonderful dinner by the Mouth of the Rock River. It was a perfect night. We could not have asked for better weather, food, or company. Our original plan was to stop for ice cream after dinner, but there was no room left. So we got home and comfy and watched a movie.

Day Eighty-Four – New Carlisle, Indiana
(8/22/2017)

It was a great day for a ride. We started off on 90, and decided we were not in the mood for another day on the expressway. The unmanned tolls were a pain, as we did not have enough quarters in our pocket, so we had to pull over and dig. We got off on Route 20 which goes through small towns all the way home, and somehow missed a turn and were heading into the city of Chicago. So we found a road and headed south to miss the city. We did find a few Harley dealers in our wandering, so it was mandatory to stop at them, one in Illinois and one in Indiana. Of course, we got pins from both. After a while, we realized that we were not getting anywhere very fast and our goal was to make it to my cousin Laura and Steve's house, so back to the highway it was. We have not seen them since the beginning of our trip at Ohio Bike Week.

The detour was fun, but not fast. We finally made it to Laura and Steve's and they had a party waiting for us. It was so good to see everyone! Of course, Laura, being the perfect host, had tons of food made and waiting. I am so blessed to have the family I have. I truly love them all. After keeping Laura and Steve up way past their bedtime, (some people still have to work in the morning), we headed up to bed for a good night's sleep. Today was another great day, so tomorrow we will get up and do it again. Amen.

Day Eighty-Five – Mentor, Ohio
(8/24/2017)

The day started out great. We left early (for us) and hit Route 20. Laura lives right where the time change is, so we are back on NY time, which means we lost an hour. Route 20 is a nice relaxing backroad that weaves through towns along the way. The speed is between 35 and 60 mph, ever changing, and lots to look at. Around 1:00, we decided we were not really making any miles, even though the ride was fun, so we decided to hit the highway and pound down some miles after we had lunch. We found a nice family restaurant, The Four Seasons, and enjoyed a great meal. The Ohio Turnpike (US 90) is definitely not as much fun, but we made our mark. The goal was to get to the other side of Cleveland. This sounds easy enough, until you hit the traffic jams all through the city. Stop and go. No fun in a car, and even less fun on a motorcycle. Bonz decided we would be really good at the next motorcycle rodeo in the slow competition. If nothing else, we got our practice in for it.

I have been having a little trouble with my bike when it hits a half-tank of gas; it starts bucking, and feels like you're riding on a carousel. It stops when I fill the tank. I tried some dry gas, but that made no difference. We are way too close to home to worry about this now, so we just stop for gas every 100 miles or so. I know it will need some work when we get home, so I'll save my issues for the guys at Harv's Harley Davidson as they usually do all the work on my bike, and they can fix anything. Having owned old cars most of my life, I have learned that it is always better to bring your vehicles to the same person to have work done. It always saves you in the long run. Find a shop you trust to be honest with you, and stick with them. And Harv's has always treated us very well.

Just as the traffic started to lighten up, we had to stop for gas, as the bike was bucking again. It was getting late, so we decided to quit for the night. We found a cheap motel with an extremely comfy bed at the America's Best Value Inn in Mentor and decided to quit for the night. I think I was out as soon as I hit the bed. Tomorrow is my second last day to get up and do it again. Amen.

Day Eighty-Six – Himrod, New York
(8/24/2017)

We woke up this morning and walked over to McDonald's for coffee and Egg McMuffins. The sky was not very promising. By the time we were showered and ready to pack, the rain had arrived. I called the office to arrange a late checkout and the motel was quite accommodating. By noon, the rain had dwindled to a drizzle, and the sky to the east was more promising. We packed and dressed in raingear and headed out for the day. When you are on a motorcycle, there is a magic thing that happens when you leave all dressed in raingear: the rain automatically stops. If you ever see a biker all dressed in raingear and there is no rain coming down, please thank them for making the rain go away. Raingear is more powerful than an old Indian rain dance, and hated by most bikers. I believe it is their severe distaste for raingear that gives it this magic power.

About a quarter mile down US 90, the roads dried up and all the rain disappeared. And Bonz and I looked totally ridiculous riding down the highway fully dressed in our glow-in-the-dark outfits for the next hour until we stopped and removed them happily from our bodies. Luckily for us, as ridiculous as we looked in our raingear, the dance with the rainclouds worked. The day was cool, but with a coat, it was a beautiful day to take a ride.

We finally got off route 90 when we hit the New York boarder. We took Route 86, which was nice and empty, for about another 200 miles before we got to ride the backroads to my sister Heather's cottage on Seneca Lake. It has been three months since we have been in New York State. There is something very exciting and also a little sad about returning home after a long trip away. At least we still have one more day of adventure to enjoy before our journey comes to an end. Route 86 is absolutely beautiful with the mountains filled with trees. We stopped at the welcome center in Chautauqua, and the view was breathtaking, overlooking Lake Chautauqua. It used to be a beautiful summer spot in the 1800s when train travel was so popular, and is still highly frequented.

I did not notice how much I missed trees until I saw them covering everything for as far as the eye can see. In just one more month, all these trees will put on the most beautiful show, with all the leaves bursting with different colors. If you have never seen a fall in the eastern part of the United States, you must put it on your bucket list as it is one of the most beautiful things you will ever see. I once read that the reds in the leaves can only be seen in this area and in China. That's it. Two places in the world. Having never traveled to China, and being a New Yorker born and raised, I highly suggest seeing the reds, golds, yellows, and oranges in the eastern United States.

We made it to Heather's around 7:30 and she had dinner all waiting for us. My sister Sue and her friend Ester are also here with her daughter Tori and her honey, Brad. We had a wonderful dinner with friends and family, which ended with a bonfire and a movie. My nieces, Gianna and Katy Jane, joined us from New Jersey after midnight. There is nothing like family, and I am truly blessed with a very large one. So good night for now; as tomorrow is another day, so we can get up and do it again. Amen.

Day Eighty-Seven – Fairport, NY
(8/26/2017)

We woke up at the lake, and spent a fun-filled day with family. But it was time to get back to our crazy life, so we headed out for our final ride for this trip. The Finger Lakes are so beautiful, and the roads home are all backroads. The day was as beautiful as the ride.

We arrived home and were met by our roommate Gary, and Bro Joe and Hell, who live on the other side of our two-family home. We settled in to a movie and a nice fire in the fireplace. There is no place like home.

I would like to thank Bonz for allowing his crazy wife to drag him all over the country on two wheels, and everyone else for all your funny and helpful suggestions on really cool places to stop. This journey was so much fun; I would do it again in a heartbeat. There is so much more to discover in this wonderful country. If you have a dream, I highly suggest putting some effort into making it come true. Life is the journey, and not necessarily the destination. Thank you for joining us on our journey, one day at a time.

Assessing changes in our fourth quarter on the road:
Observations and speculations: (days 66-87)

Sturgis was fun but the greed and profiling habits of the police department will keep us from coming back to the rally again. The rally was fun and a lot of people put a lot of work into it. It is a shame, but I prefer to go places where I am welcome. I am an old lady who has not had a drink in 19 years, and don't like being threatened by the police just because I am on a motorcycle. I guess they are having trouble leaving old stereotypes behind.

The Native American history we learned while traveling in the Black Hills was fascinating. We stopped at Little Big Horn Battlefield. It is a national monument that is half on reservation land and half on BLM land. The impressive thing about this battlefield is that they actually allow both sides of the story. Bonz is part Native American and seeing his reaction to the history was touching. I think we may have to add this kind of thing to our future rides. No matter how long you are with a person, there are always new things to learn. The only battlefield that gets more visitors than Little Big Horn is Gettysburg, Va., and they tell both perspectives too. In hearing both sides, you get a much clearer picture of what really happened.

Our mojo seems to have changed after Sturgis. As we head down route 90 towards home, I think we are very ready to be home. We've ended up on the thruway almost all the way home. We also have destinations that we are planning to stop at. So the laidback meandering we have been doing all over the US has turned into more of a destination-driven ride. We put in more miles each day, mainly on the thruway. Although our destinations are full of fun and family, the trip is a lot harder. There is nothing wrong with a destination ride; it's just that it is a little tighter on the timeline, leaving less time to play on travel days.

When we start to talk of home, we talk of all the things that we will have to do when we get there. Things like changes I would like to make to the house, how we took down two trees that need to be cut and split for winter, and of course, going back to work. There is also good talk of home, like seeing our friends again and sleeping in our own bed. This trip has opened up the lines of communication between us. Sometimes you get so used to a person that you have a tendency to not hear them anymore. You assume you already know everything about them and your learning curve is over. This trip has helped us to learn that there is a lot more to discover about each other, making our relationship fresh again. I do believe that changing everything around us daily will have a nice mellowing effect on us when we get home and have to face the changes there that we have no control over. I'm not sure we will ever get the chance to run away and just have fun for another three months, but if we win the lottery, we are out of here!

This quarter we successfully spent $700 on food, $2000 on lodging, $450 on gas, and $1300 on incidentals, bringing our grant total for this quarter to $4650. See, when you put your mind to it, you can still shop even when there is no more room to tie it down. This brings our total to a little under $17000. We left with $20,000 because it was important to us to enjoy our trip and not have to worry about finances. Just in case there was a problem, we also brought along a credit card for emergencies. Backup in any new situation is always a must.

Spending three months balancing on a motorcycle through different terrains and wind conditions can really help you realize the importance of balance in your life. The long trip has brought us closer to each other and taught us "old farts" how to play again. Traveling with your partner can show you just what it was about them that attracted you to them in the first place. New friends show up daily, and our schedules are only suggestions, allowing us to unplug from our daily routine and really live in the here and now. This re-discovery can be a lot of fun. We had no real plan, no reservations, just trusting and listening to each other and our adventure unfolded perfectly!

Since we have gotten home and back to work, we now plan out play days just as we did on the road. I have learned that work and chores will always be there, so most of them can be put off for a day of play. Learning how to keep our stress levels down will be a new focus at home. Removing the stress of everyday life has made it easier to check on what we are both feeling and thinking, and I'm afraid that adding it back will make it way too easy to slip right back into our old roles. Communicating our fears on the road helped us to stop worrying about what the future may bring, and kept our focus on what is right in front of us. Hopefully we can continue to keep this attitude and learn to add more play into our lives. Maybe it is time to take a new look at our surroundings where we live and start to discover some of the "things to do" around our own area and continue to play tourists for a bit. Life is way too short to forget to play, while learning to live our new life one day at a time.

About the Author

Hollie has always had a love for Harley Davidson motorcycles and has wanted to blend this passion with her interest in travel. After both of her children moved out of the family home Hollie had the opportunity to fulfill one of her dreams, to travel across the United States on her Harley, with her husband, Bonz. Hollie resides in Rochester, New York and when she cannot ride her Harley in the winter she spends her time reading and planning new adventures. She is often heard saying it is not about the destination but all about the journey. She would love to hear your opinion so please write a review of her book, good or bad. Suggestions are always welcome. You can also reach her at hschinzing@gmail.com. She has already started on her next book about being a female in the biker world, but does not expect this one to be out for a few years, because really good things in life take time.

Made in United States
North Haven, CT
12 September 2023

41436847R00080